# THE Book on Storytelling

## *How to Increase Your Impact, Influence and Income with the Power of Stories*

### By Michael Davis,

### *the Storytelling MD*

First Printing: 2015

ISBN 978-1-57074-182-1

Published by
Braughler Books LLC
braughlerbooks.com

To every man and woman who has the courage
to stand before other people and
share your story. Keep standing up and speaking
because *you* have a story
that *someone* needs to hear.

# What other people are saying about *THE Book on Storytelling…*

"From the very beginning of time, we have been telling stories. Stories are engaging, motivating, compelling, memorable. That's why everyone must read Michael Davis' '*THE Book on Storytelling.*' It is an **amazing cornucopia of tips and ideas** he has collected over the years from some of the best in the field.

The title says it all. This is **THE book on storytelling**. There are 52 chapters, each a gem. What follows each chapter is a "Recommended Resource." This alone is worth the price of the book.

**I can guarantee you it is THE best.** And I've read them all."

**Jerold Panas**, Author & Storyteller
'*Power Questions*' (co-author)

"Storytelling is one of the most highly rated and undervalued skills that all professionals need to develop. Mastering this skill is not a choice.

Michael Davis has been an active, long-time member of the World Champions Edge speaking community. In *'THE Book on Storytelling'* he has simplified what he has learned from the best storytelling techniques and presented them in an easy-to-use format. When you apply the lessons in this book **your presentation impact will increase."**

**Patricia Fripp**
Partner, *World Champions Edge;* Past President, *National Speakers Association*

"Facts, figures and data are commodities of the information age. The one tool that can make your messages memorable is a well-told story.

Michael Davis has demystified the ancient art and skill of storytelling and made it accessible to the masses. *'THE Book on Storytelling'* is a cookbook that **reveals the secrets** of master storytellers.

Michael has invested hundreds of hours in this well-researched book so that you don't have to. He has extracted the essential storytelling elements and placed them at the tips of your fingers.

Apply these lessons and processes and audiences will **talk about your presentations for years to come**."

**"This book is outstanding! It will be my new #1 storytelling resource."**

**Ed Tate,** CSP
*2000 World Champion of Public Speaking*

"Human beings thrive in the presence of connection. The #1 way to connect, without question, is through storytelling. Regardless of your profession, Michael Davis's book gives you a step-by-step blueprint to become a **more influential communicator** through the power of storytelling. If you follow his coaching, **you will become a great storyteller!**"

**Jeff Bloomfield**, Author
*'Story Based Selling'*

"Storytelling is at the heart of all communication. Most people think they are good storytellers. They are not. We can all learn something that can make us better and more influential. Michael Davis has compiled powerful storytelling lessons in *THE Book on Storytelling*. **Devour it.** "

**Darren LaCroix,** CSP
*2001 World Champion of Public Speaking*


"If you are a speaker looking to improve your storytelling skills, **this is the book for you.** World Class Speaker Michael Davis shows you how to develop and deliver masterful stories that are sure to keep your audiences on the **edge of their seats**. This excellent collection of tools and action steps is sure to **take your storytelling to the next level.**"

**Mitch Meyerson,** Co-Founder of *World Class Speaking* and Author of *'Mastering Online Marketing'*

"Michael Davis' *'THE Book on Storytelling'* is a well researched documentary and commentary on the value and importance on the use of effective story telling as a public speaker. He has compiled a wide assortment of information from an impressive stable of industry experts and experienced speakers and coupled it with his own experience providing the reader with both **a great depth and breadth of experience.**

His work will be **a valuable resource** to anyone wishing to expand their ability to **connect with and impact** an audience."

**Lance Miller**
*2005 World Champion of Public Speaking*

"This book has **more concrete advice** than **any** storytelling book I've read. And I've read them all."

**Paul Smith,** Bestselling Author
*'Lead with a Story'* and *'Parenting with a Story'*

"Story telling is an art, but behind it, there is a science and Michael Davis captures that brilliantly. He breaks the art of storytelling into bite-sized chunks so that anyone who's interested in learning the art and science of it can become a fabulous storyteller. I love every chapter name - they are clever and creative, and draw you in as if there is a story inside them. There is no better way to not only get a point across, but to make it memorable than with a story. Michael is Masterful and **this book is THE BOOK** when it comes to Storytelling."

**W. Roger Salam,** Best-selling Author & Speaker
Founder of *'Winners' Circle Mastermind'*


"Take Michael's advice and have a message - it worked for me, it worked for him, and **it'll work for you!"**

**Judy Carter,** comedienne and Author
*'The Message of You'* and *'Stand-Up Comedy: The Book'*

# Foreword

I woke up in a hotel in Mysore, India to a great surprise. On the previous day I had spoken at the Infosys Campus and told a story with the takeaway phrase, "Your dream is not for sale." As I crept out of bed, I saw a newspaper that had been placed under my hotel room door. I noticed a rather large picture of me on the front page. However, what pleased me the most was the headline at the top of the paper. It read, "Your Dream is Definitely Not For Sale."

I was so excited, not for the press about me, but for the fact that they remembered and even repeated my message. After all, that's one of the main reasons to speak in the first place. You must be remembered and repeated in order to be effective. What's the absolute best way to accomplish this? **Storytelling.**

If I had never told that story, they would never have remembered my message. Think back to the stories you were told as a child. Do you remember the 'Boy Who Cried Wolf?' What was the moral? Chances are you haven't read or heard that story in many years but you still remember the point. It probably even affected, even if just in some small way, the way you live. **Stories change lives.**

The fastest and most surefire way to become an excellent and highly effective presenter is to **master the art of storytelling.** If you can tell your story and make your point, you will be light-years ahead of what most presenters can do. You will...

- Stand out from the crowd

- Be remembered and repeated

- Be in-demand whether you're a speaker, teacher, salesperson, community leader, executive, manager, politician, parent, student, etc.

- Generate lucrative opportunities that lead to significant increases in income

- Thoroughly enjoy giving presentations because of the deep impact you'll make on each audience

- Make headlines of your own!

If storytelling is the key, Michael Davis is the locksmith. He holds the keys to your success in storytelling. *'THE Book on Storytelling'* will fundamentally change the way you see storytelling. As a result, more open doors will open to you than you ever thought possible.

I've met some coaches who show you *how* to discover your story. I've met others who show you how to *develop* it. Still I've met others who show you how to *deliver* it. However, Michael Davis is the ONLY one I've met who shows you how to do **all three**! He's truly the one-stop-shop for remarkable stories. **Each one of these 52 tools will help you capture the hearts and minds of your audience and touch their lives in a significant way.**

For example, let's take a look at one key called the *Then, Now, and How* formula. This formula will not only keep your audience hooked and on the edge of their seats, it will also get them to take the exact next step you want them to take. I've personally used it to sell a product that brings in an **extra 6 figure income every year**. That's right. One formula can lead to an additional 6 figure income.

Consider another key Michael gives. It's called *The Heart of Your Story*. Once you find out what this key is and follow Michael's advice on how to use it effectively, it will pump life into every story you give. More importantly, it will pump life into **every audience you have**. This key is what makes your presentations and your audiences come alive!

If you want more impact, more influence, and more income, *'THE Book on Storytelling'* is an absolute must. The world loves stories and cherishes the storytellers. Why? Because people are suffering from a daily avalanche of too much information and they need a way to filter through it. Hence, they look to stories as shortcuts. Who wins in this cluttered new age? Storytellers.

Once you pick up Michael's keys, don't be surprised to find yourself waking up in a hotel room somewhere around the world and finding that your story is being remembered and repeated. After all, you've learned from the best.

Here's to touching lives,

Craig Valentine
1999 World Champion of Public Speaking
Co-Author, #1 Amazon.com Bestseller, World Class Speaking In Action

# Table of Contents

Introduction

**Part 1 – Understanding Why You Should Tell Stories and Where to Discover Your *Stand OUT!* Stories**

1. Why Tell Stories?

2. 3D Storytelling

3. Discover Your Story, Part 1 – Uncover Your Most Meaningful Stories

4. Discover Your Story, Part 2 – Your Story File

5. The Six Common Emotions

6. Tell Your Stories … *Well*

7. Why You?

8. How YOUR Story Can Change Lives

9. Which Story Should You Tell NOW?

10. Peers Can Steer You Clear

11. Storytelling Lessons from the First Knight

# Introduction

"Daddy, read me a book."

If you're a parent, you've probably heard those words countless times. When my son, Brenden, was small, he said those words to me every night. I would scan his bookshelf and pull out books by Dr. Seuss or "Mother Goose" or "Morris the Moose." I read all of those books so many times that I could almost recite them word-for-word.

Why do children love stories? When I ask audiences that question, I hear a range of answers:

"Stories are entertaining, Mike."
"Kids learn best through repetition."
"He's just trying to put off going to sleep."

All of these answers are correct, of course. Children love stories for the same reasons adults do – they're entertaining. But properly told, stories can also be educational and memorable, and they can leave a lasting impact on audiences.

Human beings have always told stories. Before the written word was invented, stories were the only means of passing on lessons from one generation to the next. Evidence of their importance can be found all over the world, from cave drawings to Aesop's Fables to modern day golfers who spin tall tales at the country club about their prowess at the game.

Research has proven that our brains are "wired" for stories. They help us create deeper emotional connections, make it easier for us to remember lessons, and they entertain us. Stories bind us to our past and serve as a foundation for future generations.

According to an old adage in the speaking world, "If you want to make a point, tell a story. Make another point, tell another story." With this in mind, why do most people ignore stories, and instead resort to statistics and figures to sell their messages?

My fellow World Class Speaking Coach Deidre Van Nast has pointed out that these people probably loved stories when they were younger, too. It's doubtful that at bedtime they said to their parents, "Mommy, Daddy, I don't want a book tonight. Gimme some research about Goldilocks and the three bears. What was the temperature variation of the porridge she ate? Do you have some data about the structural integrity of those chairs or focus group feedback on the proper punishment she should have received for breaking and entering? And could you put that in a

PowerPoint presentation for me? Please, Mommy and Daddy, please?"

Somewhere along the line, these purveyors of statistics and data forgot that stories are the best way to learn. But it isn't enough to just let go of the statistics and tell any old story. Have you ever listened to someone go on and on and on, seemingly without a point? Did you wonder, "Why am I listening to this?"

That's because there is one important word missing from that sage advice about making your point with a story, and the word is: well. Tell a story, yes, but you have to tell it well.

Hall of Fame speaker and executive speech Patricia Fripp says, "Your audience will not remember what you say, but what they see in their minds. Tell stories." [i] When your story engages emotions and is relevant, people are much more likely to buy into your message. That's the ultimate benefit of mastering the art of storytelling.

Here's a question for you: Have you ever told a story with no point that left people wondering why they were listening to it?

If you have to answer yes to that question, you're not alone. Most people have yet to learn the art of effective storytelling. As a result, their stories don't have the impact they could have. Luckily, contrary to popular belief, great speakers and storytellers aren't born, they're made. They use a set of proven processes that create audience interest, keep their attention, and compel them to take action. And these can be learned.

At first glance, the title of this book - **THE Book on Storytelling** - may seem a bit arrogant. Who am I, a little-known speaker and author, to make the claim of writing THE book about this important topic?

If this was just a collection of *my* ideas and opinions, it would be arrogant. Fortunately, that's not what this book is.

What is it? A collection of the best ideas that I've picked up from some of the best speakers and storytellers in the world. These concepts serve as the foundation for my speech coaching and my *Stand Up, Stand OUT!* series of public speaking workshops.

Using this system, you'll benefit from the years of trial and error and tens of thousands of dollars invested by my coaches and me. Over the course of 52 chapters, you'll build one skill upon another as you master this craft.

This book is meant to be an experiential tool, a step-by-step adventure to learn how to discover, develop and deliver *Stand OUT!* stories that impact audiences and compel them to act on your message. In each chapter, you'll pick up a new 'tool' or process that builds upon previous lessons.

At the conclusion of each chapter, you'll see an ACTION Step related to what you've learned. I'm a huge believer that the best way to learn to swim is to jump in the pool and start flailing! Storytelling is no different. Actually, it's safer. If you jump in a pool and fail to swim, you might drown. If you jump in the "storytelling pool" and fail, you can just dust yourself off and try again. As speaker and author Rory Vaden has said, "Mistakes are proof that you are trying." [ii]

Don't dissect or over-think every action, just do them. Test each. Get feedback. Make adjustments. Test again. Repeat until your stories create the results you want for both you and your audience. This process has worked for Hall of Fame and World Champion speakers, it will work for you, too.

When you master this process, you can reap the following benefits:

✓ Make more money
✓ Advance your career faster

✓ Create more opportunities
✓ Develop greater confidence
✓ Become better known in your industry or community
✓ Free up more time
✓ Reduce the stress and anxiety often involved with developing stories

My promise to you is this: Devote just a few minutes to each chapter, then practice what you learn, and you'll quickly improve. Within one year, you'll be at least three times the storyteller you are today. (While this is designed to be a year-long program, if you want to go at a faster pace, go for it!)

My hope for you is that you'll make many 'mistakes' as a result of your testing out each new idea you learn. That will mean that you're taking chances, trying new ideas, and learning. As a byproduct of those mistakes, you'll become a storyteller people can't wait to hear. The key is to **keep taking action**.

An additional benefit of this process is that, as you proceed through the book, you'll gain a deeper understanding of your individual style and will become more comfortable being yourself.

Each chapter ends with a Recommended Resource. It may be an article, video, or book written by another expert. I've been asked "Why would you suggest that your readers invest in other author's materials?" Because they bring unique perspectives and insight, and make 'THE Book on Storytelling' one of the most comprehensive books available on this subject. It is meant to provide the best value in order for you to create the most impactful version of *your* stories.

Before concluding this introduction, here is your first **Action Step** (actually two):

At the end of this book, you will find *The 12 Stand OUT! Storytelling Competencies Questionnaire* in the Appendix. Complete the Questionnaire to determine the level of skill you have right now in each of the storytelling areas listed. This will help you measure your progress as you work through the book. Although it's a self-assessment, feel free to ask others if you aren't sure about your proficiency in any of these areas.

When you reach the halfway point of the book (Chapter 27), re-take the questionnaire; then again after you complete the final chapter. This will be your 'Report Card' which shows where you've had the greatest growth.

Additionally, visit the link **http://bit.ly/1xVppwx** to download your PDF copy of **THE Book on Storytelling** *Playbook*. This provides a document to record your stories, thoughts, and progress. It is an additional tool to help you gauge your growth.

As we began our journey together, remember that storytelling isn't about being perfect, it's about connecting with the people who are sitting in front of you. Craft stories from you heart and convey the messages that are most important to you, and they will Stand OUT! in the hearts of your audience.

I look forward to guiding you toward becoming a storyteller who impacts lives and leaves a lasting impression.

Always remember that **you** have a story that **someone** needs to hear.

Part 1


Understanding **Why** You Should
Tell Stories
and Where to **Discover** Your *Stand
OUT!* Stories

# Step 1 - Why Tell Stories?

Why are stories so important to us humans? The most obvious reason is that they create an emotional connection, but why is storytelling so effective in business?

In his book, *Lead with a Story*, author Paul Smith highlights 10 compelling reasons to tell stories[iii]:

**Reason 1 - Storytelling is simple.** Anyone can do it. In fact, you've been doing it since you first learned how to put sentences together and say them. You don't need a college degree to tell stories.

**Reason 2 - Storytelling is timeless.** Because human beings have always told stories, it isn't a fad, unlike many other ideas that come along in the business world. Storytelling is especially powerful for leaders, and it always will be.

**Reason 3 - Stories are demographic-proof.** Everybody - regardless of age, race, socio-economic status, or gender - likes to listen to stories.

**Reason 4 - Stories are contagious.** The best stories spread by word-of-mouth. Before human beings invented the written word, the only way to pass on their stories was to "tell" them. One person told another, and they were passed down through the generations. Think about stories that you've heard and then shared with others. In modern vernacular, your story can "go viral" in a few hours.

**Reason 5 - Stories are easier to remember.** According to psychologist Jerome Bruner, facts are 20 times more likely to be remembered if they are part of a story.

**Reason 6 - Stories inspire.** Have you ever heard someone walk out of a business meeting and say, "Wow! You'll never believe the PowerPoint presentation I just saw!" Probably not, because most of the people walking out of a PowerPoint presentation are just rushing to get coffee and wake up.

You *have*, however, heard people say *"Wow, I just heard this great story!"* It's why top-selling movies and books become popular.

**Reason 7 - Stories appeal to all types of learners.** In any group, about two out of five people will be predominantly visual learners. They learn best from videos, diagrams, or illustrations. Another two out of five will be auditory. They learn best through the spoken word, such as lectures or discussions. The remaining one out of five people is kinesthetic, learning best by doing, experiencing, or feeling.

The best stories have aspects that work for all three types of learners. Visual learners appreciate the mental pictures that your story creates. Auditory learners focus on words and the storyteller's voice. Kinesthetic learners remember the emotional connections and feelings from a story.

**Reason 8 - Stories fit better where most of the learning happens in the workplace.** According to communications expert Evelyn Clark, "Up to 70 percent of the new skills, information and competence in the workplace is acquired through 'informal learning'" [iv] such as what happens in team settings, mentoring, and peer-to-peer communication. And the bedrock of informal learning is storytelling.

**Reason 9 - Stories put the listener in a learning mode**. According to bestselling author and training coach Margaret Parkin, storytelling "re-creates in us that emotional state of curiosity which is ever present in children, but which as adults we tend to lose. Once in this childlike state, we tend to be more receptive and interested in the information we are given." [v]

Author and organizational narrative expert David Hutchens points out, "Storytelling puts listeners in a different orientation. They put their pens and pencils down, they open up their posture, and just listen." [vi]

**Reason 10 - Telling stories shows respect for the audience.** Stories get your message across without arrogantly telling listeners what to think or do. Regarding what to think, storytelling author Annette Simmons observed, "Stories give people freedom to come to their own conclusions. People who reject predigested conclusions might just agree with your interpretations if you get out of their face long enough for them to see what you have seen." [vii]

To underscore the reason *why* to tell stories, especially in the workplace, corporate storyteller David Armstrong suggests, "If there was ever a time when you could just order people to do something [at work], it has long since passed. Telling a story, where you underline the moral, is a great way of explaining to people what needs to be done, without saying, 'Do this!'" [viii] This answers the question "Why?"

**ACTION STEP:** Begin a new habit by recording stories from your life. Don't censor. Write down whatever stories comes to mind, no matter how minor or major. Don't be concerned about the sequence of the stories either. Just record them.

If you do this every day for 30 days, you'll develop a habit that will create a treasure trove of story material.

**RECOMMENDED RESOURCE:** The book, *Lead with a Story,* written by Paul Smith. Paul is a former executive at Procter & Gamble. He interviewed 100 worldwide corporate leaders to determine how they use stories to lead their companies. There are great examples that you can use as models, especially for business presentations. To get your copy, visit: http://amzn.to/1ud9FRk.

# Step 2 - **3D Storytelling**

Did you see the movie, "Avatar"? If so, did you see it in a theater? I'll never forget the night I saw the film, just a few days after Christmas. I had heard all the buzz, but as I slipped on my 3D glasses, I was skeptical.

Within a few minutes, that skepticism was replaced by awe. Director James Cameron had created a visual masterpiece, one that made me feel like I was *in* the movie. The experience struck me so deeply, I walked out of the theater and knew that, as a speaker, that was the type of experience I wanted to create for my audiences. "Avatar" and stories like it are the root of a concept called 3-dimensional (or 3D) Storytelling.

In the world of computers and film, 3D refers to the concept of creating an illusion of depth perception. The result is a 'you are there' experience. 3D Storytelling is designed to develop a presentation that impacts people long after they hear you speak. The benefit is twofold: It helps the audience, and also creates more opportunities for you. Like a great movie, word will spread, and others will want to hear your message. Unlike the movies, your audience will not be required to wear those obnoxious glasses (unless, of course, you want to add that uniqueness to your presentation).

So, what is 3D Storytelling? It's a three-step process conceived by my business partner, Jamey French. It is a formula which guides you to *Discover, Develop and Deliver* your unique stories. Actually, there is a fourth D—*Depth*. The remainder of this book will center on the 3D process. You'll discover stories with depth that connect with audience's emotions. You'll develop stories with depth that capture and keep your audience's attention. You'll deliver your stories with a level of depth that makes others feel as if they are part of the story.

The end result of this is a more impactful message and you will feel a greater level of confidence, creativity, and conviction in your ability to tell meaningful stories. This will lead to improved leadership abilities, faster advancement for your career, and higher income, and many other benefits.

How can I make this claim? I've seen it work. The process has propelled my career and the careers of many others. If we did it, so can you.

One other benefit of this program is that 3D Storytelling is a repeatable process. Many speech coaches will help you create a story, and if you need help with another speech at a later date, you can rehire that coach again. There's nothing wrong with that approach, but do you want to be dependent on another person to create every one of your presentations?

The 3D approach is similar to the proverb "Give a man a fish, and you feed him for a day. Teach a man to fish, and you feed him for a lifetime." You are about to learn a format that you can repeat over and over. (With all respect to the previous proverb, the process doesn't discriminate. It isn't just for men.)

Let's dive in. In your next lesson, you'll be introduced to the First Dimension of 3D Storytelling, how to *Discover Your Story*.

**ACTION STEP:** Your assignment is to watch at least two movies or two TV shows that you enjoy. Alternatively, you can review a couple of your favorite books. See if you recognize repeatable patterns in the stories – plot structure, theme, or genre are just three of the many types of patterns you might recognize. Patterns which appeal to you may serve as keys to your own stories.

**RECOMMENDED RESOURCE:** Visit YouTube and watch two short speeches: one from World Champion speaker Jim Key and the other from the great speaker Tony Robbins. Their stories create an experience for the audience. Notice how each speaker masterfully wraps his story around a foundational message:

To watch Jim Key's speech, "Never Too Late," click here: http://bit.ly/1r1ZxJ5. To watch Tony Robbins' speech, "The Story Behind Rocky and Sylvester Stallone's Success," click here: http://bit.ly/1r1ZI73.

# Step 3 - **Discover Your Story, Part 1 –** *Uncover Your Most Meaningful Stories*

Randy Harvey is the 2004 World Champion of Public Speaking. He is also an attorney, a former school administrator, and a successful professional speaker. Most importantly (for our purposes) he's a passionate student of the art of public speaking. He offers a unique perspective that can help you as you dive deeply into your stories.

Before Randy agrees to work with someone on their presentations, he asks them to consider three important questions. They (and you) may never be able to fully answer them. In his words, "you will continually answer these questions for the rest of your life, gaining a deeper understanding of the questions." [ix]

Carefully give these questions thought as you prepare your stories. Your answers will help you develop messages that resonate deeply with audiences. They will also help you be remembered long after you speak.

**Question #1 –** *Who are you?* Nothing like a good, metaphysical question to start you off, right? Even more than the other two, this is the question you may never fully answer. There are some additional questions that can help you answer this one:

1. *What do you most believe in?*
2. *What are the roles you play in life?*
3. *What is your philosophy of life?*
4. *Why do you do what you do?*
5. *What would the ideal you look and feel like?*

Question #1 can't be answered in just a few minutes. That's because it's meant to get to the essence of who you are. As your life changes and you experience more events, you will gain more insight into the "real you." Once you're willing to share these insights about your personality with audiences, you'll create stories that continually resonate at deeper levels.

**Question #2 - *What are you about?*** Some additional questions to help answer this one are:

1. *What are your core values?*
2. *How do you spend your time?*
3. *If time and money were not issues, what would you do with your time and your life? Who would you spend that time with? Where would you go?*
4. *Which values do you believe in so strongly that you would die for them? (For example: Freedom? Family? Love?)*

I know what you may be thinking right about now. "Michael, I just want to learn to tell stories. I just got started with this program, and you're hitting me with these deep, philosophical questions! What's up with you?"

I understand. Answering these questions will be the most difficult tasks you encounter in this course. They are placed early in the program because when you do this type of work, you are ahead of most storytellers (probably 95% or more). I promise this will pay off in big ways as you progress through the book. They are part of the foundation of your evolving storytelling skills.

The answers to this second question will unlock your core values. These are the connectors that will develop a bond with your audience and inspire them to act on your message.

**Question #3 - *Where did you learn these values?*** Who or what taught you those beliefs you hold most dear? Was it a person or persons? Was it an idea you picked up from a book? Did you hear it in a class?

Wherever it came from, it was a point of change in your life. Change is the payoff that audiences are waiting for. Your best stories will be born from this third question. The answers to this will provide the catalyst for the change you experienced and that other people might want to go through.[x]

With the insight you gain from these questions, you will also have a deeper understanding of your *WHY*. In his bestselling book, *Start With WHY,* author Simon Sinek discusses the power of correctly answering the question, "What do you do?"

Most people respond with answers like, "I'm a lawyer" or "I'm a teacher." The problem with these answers is that they don't get to the core of why you do the work you do or why you are the person you are. Attorneys probably don't get up in the morning eager to practice law. They do it to defend the wrongly accused or to prevent injustice. Most teachers are motivated more by the idea of molding young minds and helping kids reach their full potential.

Mr. Sinek believes that when you first answer the question by explaining why you do something, you create a deeper emotional connection and develop longer-term relationships.

This is also true with storytelling. When you answer the three questions in this lesson, you begin to understand yourself better, including why you do what you do. You will have a deeper understanding of your true nature—the "real you."

With this new knowledge, you'll be able create stories that won't simply entertain; they'll impact others and change the way they think, feel, or act. Ultimately, that is why you stand up and speak to any audience. It's the greatest gift you can give them.

**ACTION STEP**: Answer Randy Harvey's three questions. Remember, this is just the first step in a journey of deeper self-discovery. Once you start the process, you'll want to go back again and again to understand yourself in new ways. If ever an exercise proved the Chinese proverb, "A journey of a thousand miles begins with a single step," it's this one.

**RECOMMENDED RESOURCE:** The book previously mentioned in this lesson, *Start With WHY,* by Simon Sinek. This is not a book about speaking or storytelling, but it's a terrific next step to follow the lesson in this chapter.

Mr. Sinek has changed the points of view of people all around the world with this classic work. Once you understand your own "why," your influence and impact on others will change dramatically. To get your copy, visit: http://amzn.to/1i65OV3. If you'd like to watch Mr. Sinek's highly rated YouTube video, *Start With Why,* visit: http://bit.ly/1r1ZTiO.

# Step 4 - **Discover Your Story, Part 2 –** *Your Story File*

A common question coaching clients ask is, "What are the popular subjects?" On the surface, this seems like a reasonable question. If you can discover the hot topics, especially those that people will pay for, why not talk about those?

Dig a little deeper, though, and you'll discover that this is not the best method to choose your topic. Why? Think about a presentation you've heard where the speaker clearly wasn't an expert and/or had little passion. Did you get the full benefit of that talk?

Probably not. An expert, or someone with a deep interest in the subject, would be a much better choice to present that material.

The key to uncovering your subject matter—your storytelling gold, if you will—is to review the stories that have most impacted your life. One of the best pieces of advice about choosing your subject comes from Mark Brown, Toastmasters 1995 World Champion of Public Speaking. He asks the question, "If this was your last day on Earth, what advice would you want to share with a favorite child in your life?"

That's a powerful question and an equally powerful exercise. In the five-step process that follows, you will uncover your most important and influential stories.

To begin, create a new storytelling file with five columns. Record the following information in each:

**Column One:** Write down or type the most important lessons you've learned in your life. Don't edit at this point; simply record them. Examples of this could be: *The Importance of Persistence; Be Kind to Others; Spend Money Wisely; Don't Steal.*

Then, ask friends and family the most important lessons they've learned. Some of them may resonate with you. Add those to your list. There is no limit to the number of ideas you can add.

**Column Two**: Document the stories associated with the lessons in column one. Keep in mind that stories can connect to more than one message. For example, a story about your grandfather, who succeeded in business after many failed attempts and also treated every person he met with respect and fairness, could lead to messages about persistence or treating people with dignity. Again, don't edit at this point; record every important story in your life.

**Column Three:** Record the emotions created by those stories. World Champion of Public Speaking David Brooks has noted that human beings share six basic emotions: *Happiness, Anger, Sadness, Disgust, Fear,* and *Surprise.* [xi] You may have experienced one, two, or all six of these for each story. Just as you did in the first two columns, don't edit this information.

**Column Four:** Include all of the characters involved in your tale. Note that characters don't always have to be human beings. Animals can play a crucial role in your story. I've even heard great stories in which inanimate objects like books or cars were brought to life and became integral to the teaching of the main message. If some one or some thing is important to selling your message, put it in column four.

**Column Five:** Record the change that occurred in your life because of the incident. This is crucial to your story if it's going to have a lasting impact. Without change, the story doesn't provide benefit to your audience.

The types of changes you or other characters experience can be endless. An illness could have changed the amount of time you now spend with family or friends; a job promotion may have altered your view of persistence; or a bankruptcy might have adjusted how you manage money.

You now have the next version of one of your most important tools—your Story File. This will be a source you continually refer to and use to create your most impactful presentations.

You should continually add to this file. Long-forgotten stories will come to mind at a later time, while some that are meaningful now will likely lose their impact over time. Others with little importance now may become more significant later.

This lesson is a critical step in the Discovery process. Your work in this chapter will be more in-depth. The time you put in is well worth the effort. This is a foundational step. Your story file can become a source which you can refer to when you have a last minute request to speak, when you need material for a keynote address, or when you're looking for a topic for a speech contest.

**ACTION STEP:** Create the first version of your Story File. Use the 5-step process discussed in this lesson.

**RECOMMENDED RESOURCE:** The book *Did I Ever Tell You About the Time..."* by Grady Jim

Robinson. Grady Jim is a legendary speaker with a wealth of stories. His messages resonate deeply with audiences. Study this book, and you'll better understand how to weave emotions into your stories. To get your copy, visit: http://amzn.to/1lIczyc.

# Step 5 - **The Six Common Emotions**

The first time you heard the fable of the tortoise and the hare, you were probably surprised by the outcome. "There's no way that tortoise could beat the hare!" When you first saw the movie "Jaws," you were probably afraid to go back in the ocean. "I'm not going out there where a great white can have me for a tasty afternoon snack!"

When you read *The Diary of Anne Frank*, you no doubt felt anger at the plight of Anne's family and surprise by the insight of a teenage girl who, despite her tragic circumstances, concluded, "I still believe, in spite of everything, that people are really good at heart."

Stories have the power to move us in a way that facts and figures cannot. For example, history books will tell you that millions of lives were lost during the Holocaust. As terrible as those numbers are, it's hard to emotionally grasp the significance of so many people gone. When individual stories from that time period are told, however, they can stir your emotions at a deep level.

The insight of a girl like Anne Frank or the heroic efforts of Oskar Schindler, who saved the lives of over 1,200 (and was portrayed in the movie "Schindler's List") resonate with audiences, and they're remembered years after they're told.

Even the simplest of stories can connect if they stir feelings in the listener. So, how can you ensure that your stories connect emotionally? Tie them into common experiences. Remember the six most common emotions: Happiness, Anger, Sadness, Disgust, Fear, and Surprise. Without exception, every effective story I've heard strikes a chord with at least one of these.

The power of story goes beyond tapping into the six common emotions, though. The ultimate benefit of many stories is providing the audience with *hope*. This may be the greatest gift you can give anybody. The "Star Wars" films at their core are about redemption. The movie "It's a Wonderful Life" is about the value of every person's life. "Titanic" offers the belief that love can conquer time and death itself. *Hope.*

Legendary Hollywood screenwriter Robert McKee has said, "Given the choice between trivial material brilliantly told versus profound material badly told, an audience will always choose the trivial told brilliantly" [xii] How can your story be well-told? Start with the six emotions.

You don't have to be a famous author or Hollywood director to impact lives. In a world that too often focuses on negativity, your stories can provide the hope that others need. Tap into the human desire to hear stories, wrap them around meaningful messages, tie in at least one of the six common emotions, and you will take a huge step to becoming a presenter who inspires others to change the way they think, feel, or act.

**ACTION STEP**: Review the stories in your story file and determine how you can add more emotions created by each. The more feelings generated, the more likely you'll connect with your audience at a deeper level.

**RECOMMENDED RESOURCE:** The book *Story: Substance, Style and the Principles of Screenwriting* by Robert McKee. Mr. McKee is a legendary Hollywood screenwriter who is widely known for his popular "Story Seminar."

This book isn't just for screenwriters. Speakers and presenters in many fields attend his workshop and seek his expertise. He will expand your knowledge of the storytelling genre so that you'll never watch TV or movies the same. Put his tools and ideas to good use, and your audiences will never see you the same either. To get your copy, visit: http://amzn.to/1sTyUqT.

# Step 6 - Tell Your Stories ... *Well*

Think about the typical speaker. S/he stands before a group and gives a talk based on what? That's right, facts and figures. If you're having a really good day, that information is printed onto a series of PowerPoint slides in 8-point font with overlapping graphs.

Remember this phrase: **Stories connect; facts and figures disconnect.**

This isn't a lesson about avoiding facts and figures entirely. Sometimes, they can be an important part of a presentation. The point is that if you choose not to be like most speakers, always include well-crafted stories, and you will stand out from the crowd.

In the Introduction to this book, you were introduced to a speaking adage created by the late Bill Gove, founder of the National Speakers Association. "If you want to make a point, tell a story. Make another point, tell another story." That is great wisdom and excellent advice. With all the respect in the world for Mr. Gove, I would add one word to his suggestion, however. That word is "well." To make a point, tell your story *well.*"

Have you ever heard a story that left you wondering "What is this guy talking about? Why should I care?" If you haven't, you're the only one. More importantly, have *you* ever told a story that left others wondering, "What are you talking about?" and "Why should I care?" If your answer is "no," you aren't telling enough stories. Every one of us, at some point, has told a story that didn't go over well.

My client, Patti, was a self-confessed "rambler." When she learned that I'm a speaking coach, she excitedly said, "Michael, I really need your help. I've agreed to give a keynote speech for the Chamber, and I'm waking up every day nauseated just thinking about it. I've got knots in my stomach. "I'm 65; I'm too old to have morning sickness!"

She slowed down and with a sigh, added, "They've only given me 25 minutes to speak, and I don't think I can do it. I *know* I talk too much. I can't stay focused, and when I end the monthly meetings at my organization, people are s-o-o-o relieved. Can you help me?"

Patti wasn't scheduled to give her keynote speech for another 11 ... *months!* She was looking at the possibility of nearly a year of Alka Seltzer, sleepless nights, and "morning sickness."

Fortunately, Patti avoided that fate. On the night she gave her speech, she finished in three minutes less than her allotted time, received a standing ovation, and got donations of time and money for her organization. What allowed her to experience such a dramatic shift?

She learned many of the tools and processes that you will learn in the coming chapters and became a speaker who harnesses the power of story to change lives. One way to inspire with a story is to create a compelling vision of the future. It's what makes a leader others follow rather than someone who is quickly forgotten.

President John Kennedy is a case in point. In 1962, he stood before a crowd of over 40,000 people in Rice Stadium in Texas and laid out an ambitious goal for the United States. "We choose to go to the moon. We choose to go to the moon in this decade and do the other things, not because they are easy, but because they are hard, because that goal will serve to organize and measure the best of our energies and skills, because that challenge is one that we are willing to accept, one we are unwilling to postpone, and one which we intend to win, and the others, too."

Is this a story in the traditional sense? Technically, no, but it's certainly a vision of the future. And that vision tells a story of millions of Americans working together with the common goal of winning a race to be the first to another celestial body to advance the world technologically.

President Kennedy could have said, "Our goal is to be the first to send a man to the moon and return him safely. As you can see on this chart, we'll be funding this with a $25 billion investment. This graph shows an increasing workforce that will plateau at over 300,000, and we will accomplish this goal in 7-1/2 years, which is the equivalent of 36,000,000 total man-hours."

Although the numbers are correct, would they have inspired the public in the way his emotional language did? Highly doubtful.

*That* is the power of story. You and I will probably never have the opportunity to set such a lofty goal as inspiring Americans to visit distant moons or planets. But our stories can still inspire others.

As you prepare your next talk, remember that to make your point, you should tell a story … *well*. In the coming chapters, you will learn more about how to do just that.

**ACTION STEP**: Take time to think about the lessons learned from the stories you've listed in your story file. For example, if the story of the tortoise and the hare resonates with you, themes such as persistence or avoiding overconfidence are probably important to you. These could be the main points of some of *your* stories.

**RECOMMENDED RESOURCE:** Watch President Kennedy's inspirational and visionary speech laying out his dream of landing Americans on the moon. Visit this link to watch: http://bit.ly/1qwyl6F.

# Step 7 - Why You?

*"Everyone is necessarily the hero of his own life story."* -- John Barth, writer

"Why would anyone listen to me? I'm just an ordinary guy from the Midwest. I've lived a pretty good life with just a few problems." Those were the words of Lance Miller, the 2005 Toastmasters World Champion of Public Speaking. At first glance, this sounds like a legitimate question. Why would anyone want to listen to a speaker who hasn't accomplished an uncommon feat or overcome great odds?

There is no doubt that hearing a well-told tale of surviving a near-fatal accident, climbing Mt. Everest, or winning Olympic Gold can be compelling. There's one problem, though. Not many people can relate to climbing the world's tallest mountain or achieving Olympic glory. It's possible to link common themes to these tales - such as overcoming adversity or the power of focusing on one goal - but few speakers effectively make those links.

The truth is that the majority of people sitting in your audience will relate more to Lance (and you and me) more than they ever will survivors of major accidents, or extraordinary achievements. That's because they haven't experienced those uncommon events. That's actually to your advantage. You can connect with them by sharing lessons learned from your day-to-day life.

For example, if you've ever been around children, you've probably felt the pain of watching a child struggle and fall while learning to ride a bicycle, or the humor of a kid lying about who broke your favorite lamp. You've experienced the joy of seeing that child overcome those same challenges.

There are various lessons that can be taken from these stories: *The Power of Persistence*; *How to Make Failure Your Greatest Ally*; or *The Power of Patience When Your Kid is Driving You Insane*. When people relate to your story, they're more open to your message.

Another way to connect with and inspire audiences to take action is to share your struggles and failures. If you're like a lot of speakers, you might feel embarrassed or afraid to publicly discuss your pain, but difficult experiences cause an audience to feel closer to you. Again, they can relate and they see you as human, like them.

For instance, early in my career as a speaker, I was insecure and unsure of myself, so I tried to be perfect each time I got up in front of an audience. I made sure my suit was impeccable, my tie was straight, and not a hair was out of place. I also tried to memorize my speeches word-for-word so that the flow of my presentation would also be perfect.

What's the problem with that? 1) Focusing on those details put my attention on me and not where it belonged—on the audience; and 2) Presenters who come across as polished or perfect don't feel real. Audiences can't relate to them because these speakers are seen as too slick.

I didn't understand this until I walked into a Toastmasters meeting one day, and I was asked to substitute for a fellow member who couldn't give his prepared speech. I was reluctant, but I accepted and gave an impromptu five-minute talk.

After the meeting, my friend, Chris, came up to me and said, "Mike, that was the best speech I've ever heard you give. It was like I was listening to the real you. Keep doing what you did today."

After that, I stopped worrying about my appearance and memorizing my talks. My focus shifted to the audience and the benefit they could receive from my message. And that has made a huge difference in responses from audiences whenever I speak. There is a connection and a sense of giving something valuable to others, even though I've never done anything extraordinary or special. I simply share my struggles and the lessons I've learned from them.

The next time you feel ordinary like Lance, embrace your "ordinary-ness" and keep this in mind: *Audiences remember the connection, not the perfection.*

Speaker Michael McKinley said it even better: "Audiences have seen smooth; they've seen slick. Don't fake who you are. When giving speeches, you can work so hard on the WHAT that you forget the WHO; which is you. The audience wants to see your vulnerability and what you've done with your failures. They want you to offer hope that they too can overcome whatever obstacles come their way." [xiii]

You have a story that someone needs to hear. Share it.

**ACTION STEP:** Record the changes you've experienced from the stories in your file. For instance, after the birth of my son, Brenden, I felt an unconditional love I had never before experienced. I became much more grounded, and for the first time in my life, became much less self-centered.

**RECOMMENDED RESOURCE:** Listen to Lance Miller's World Championship speech. This is a story that highlights how an ordinary exchange with a stranger can become a life-changing lesson. One of the best presentations you will hear.  Visit this link to watch: http://bit.ly/1A68RQK

# Step 8 - How YOUR Story Can Change Lives

What is the purpose of a story? When asked this question, audiences offer various responses. "To entertain," "to educate," "to inspire."

All of those responses are good, and there's no right or wrong answer. But there is a deeper reason. It's the thought process of the audience when you speak, the way they *Think, Feel,* or *Act* (or a combination of these).

I've mentioned those three words in previous chapters, but now, we'll focus on their importance. If you don't change at least one of these, why are you sharing your story? If your answer is, "Well, Michael, because it makes me feel good," please stop! People are way too busy today to feed your need to be seen and heard. Remember in the last lesson how I changed my focus to the benefit I could provide my audience, rather than giving the 'perfect' talk? It made all the difference!

When you provide value to others and change their perspective, you accomplish something important. You help another person live life a little bit easier. But many new speakers believe they need to tell a story with a message no one has ever heard. Guess what? That animal doesn't exist. No one, not even the best, highest-paid professional speakers have a unique subject.

If you watch the winning speeches from Toastmasters International World Championship of Public Speaking since 1990, you'll notice something interesting—several of the winners talk about the same subject. For example, 1996 Champion David Nottage, 2001 Champion Darren LaCroix, and 2010 Champion David Henderson each referred to the concept of falling down and getting back up.

What made each of those speeches special was the speakers' own stories, which made their perspectives individual, relatable, heartfelt, and genuine. Each described how he tried to overcome obstacles. The audience could relate because everyone has fallen down and struggled to get back up and keep moving forward.

This willingness to share your failures, struggles, or adversities will connect you with others much faster than sharing successes. In the last chapter, you read about the problems created when you try to be too perfect and only show your successes.

You've probably heard a speaker who stood up and told everyone how terrific he is, how great his life has been, and how, if you follow his path, you, too, can be great. When I hear these perfect people, I feel like asking someone to hand me a little white bag because I'm gonna be sick.

Not only are these stories not relatable; they aren't even believable. These people cause audience members to think, "Well, she's just special" or "He could do it, but I could never do that." And you know what? If you think that when listening to those speakers, you're right. You could probably never do what they did because they didn't do it without struggle either. It wasn't nearly as easy as it sounds. Those kinds of stories don't create warm and fuzzy feelings, do they?

Don't get me wrong: Audiences do want to know how you overcame your difficulties. They don't want to hear a long sob story with no positive outcome. They simply need you to connect with them through your struggles *first*. After you've established that connection, you can share the hope, which is how you got over the hurdle.

Also, if you're sharing stories of overcoming adversity, it's important to let the audience know that you didn't do it alone. Make other people or a process the hero of your story, not yourself. That keeps you on the audience's level and more closely connected to them.

Always remember that you change the way others *Think, Feel or Act* when you provide *hope*. They may be struggling financially, in a difficult relationship, or having problems with their kids. Your story could give them the hope they need.

**ACTION STEP:** Visit YouTube and watch a brief video called "You're a Good Poppa" by Chris Gardner. Chris was the subject of the movie "The Pursuit of Happyness." The clip focuses on a simple phrase uttered by his son in a moment when Chris was filled with doubt. It was a powerful moment. As a father, I've had days when I've wondered if I was a good Dad or a good enough provider. This simple clip reminded me that "Yeah, you've done OK." Thanks for the reminder, Chris.

After you watch, record moments in your life when someone or some event gave you hope. Why did that person or event make you feel that way? How did it change your perspective? How did it make you change the way you Think, Feel or Act? Could it provide hope to others?

Visit this link to watch: http://bit.ly/12Bpp7l.

**RECOMMENDED RESOURCE:** The book, *The Presentation Secrets of Steve Jobs*, by Carmine Gallo. Mr. Gallo has invested a great deal of time studying Jobs' presentations. He offers insight into

Jobs' thought processes, his obsessive attention to detail, and his masterful use of props. Steve Jobs was a master communicator and showman, and Mr. Gallo helps you understand why. To get your copy, visit: http://amzn.to/1ppeV1g.

# Step 9 - Which Story Should You Tell NOW?

It was June 7, 2008 at 2:15 am. If you had been sitting in the passenger seat of my car, you would have seen the look of realization on my face. I understood why I had failed. My epiphany just might help you as you choose which stories to share with your audience.

Two days earlier, I had competed in the Toastmasters International Speech contest in Ottawa, Canada. A victory in that contest would have earned me the right to participate in the World Championship of Public Speaking just two months later.

In the competition, I gave one of my favorite speeches entitled "Find Your Mud Puddle." There was energy, the audience was involved, and I had fun. I walked off stage feeling like I belonged, that I had improved as a speaker, and maybe, just maybe, I had won the contest.

Later that night, the announcements were made. The third place winner's name ... wasn't me. That's good! The second place winner was announced Again, not me. Even better! The winner was announced.

Wait a minute! Charley Wilson? That's not how I pronounce my name. It's pronounced "Mi-kul Day-vis." What? I didn't win? Oh…

It was two days later during that late night car ride back from Ottawa that I understood why I hadn't gained favor with the judges. The story I told was one of my favorites. It was a significant event in my life when my three-year old son, Brenden, taught me a valuable lesson about stress relief. There was a problem with the story, though. It was ten years old. The initial impact of the lesson had long passed.

When a message loses its freshness, it's almost as stale as a loaf of bread that's passed it's expiration date. It's hard to swallow. The emotional strength is diminished, and the audience impact is lost.

What is the lesson for you? Actually, there are two. First, you don't have to necessarily discard older stories. Just bring them into the current day and share why they're still relevant. In my case, I could have told how I'm using stress relief today, the benefits that has brought me, and how it could help others.

The second lesson is: Discard your story if you can find no current relevance in it. It may have been important to you once, but if you don't have the emotional connection to it now, there is no way your audience will feel it.

It isn't easy to set aside a favorite story. It's like giving up one of your babies. OK, maybe that's a bit extreme, but at least the story that you've lovingly created and given your heart and soul to will never talk back to you and tell you it hates you when it becomes a teenager. But I digress…

If you're willing to be honest with yourself, you'll know when a story has run its course. Speakers, like any other profession, can get caught in a comfort zone. They may be giving talks that are still *pretty* good but aren't creating the same impact they once did.

As one of my mentors, World Champion speaker Craig Valentine, has said, "Are you too good to become great? Are you willing to let go of the things that made you good, so that you can reach outside of your comfort and try to become great?"

Lessons sometimes come from unexpected sources. I never anticipated that a 1,530-mile round-trip drive would provide insight into the effect of time on my stories. As writers say, "kill your darlings" or get rid of anything that doesn't serve you anymore, no matter how much you like it. If you do that, you won't need to make a 30-

hour round trip drive to discover the impact of time on your stories.

**ACTION STEP:** Review your story file, and ask yourself if the stories still have an emotional impact on you. Define those emotions, and decide if that is what you want to share with an audience *now*. Ask other speakers if the concept of the story makes sense and if they can see the potential connection.

**RECOMMENDED RESOURCE:** Usually at this point in the lesson, you receive a suggested resource. In this chapter, however, the recommendation is to focus on your own story file. If you've completed each of the ACTION STEPS in previous chapters, you've built a healthy file of stories. Look for the ones that stand out and support the messages that have the most impact on you *today*. As you go through your file, give yourself credit for creating each story. They have all taken some work, and even if you have to let some of them go, they've all been well worth the effort.

# Step 10 - Peers Can Steer You Clear

In his classic book, *Think and Grow Rich,* Napoleon Hill introduced the concept of the Mastermind, a group of like-minded individuals who help one another achieve various goals. This concept has been used by many successful people, and it underscores the power of group thinking.

A peer storytelling group can be helpful, too. Just like in a Mastermind, you can share, evaluate, and encourage members to greater heights. In short, your peers can help you steer clear of mistakes and problems.

Where can you find prospective members for this group? Other speakers are your best choice. If you don't know many of them, look for people who present before audiences at work, or in your community, and members of Toastmasters. Let these people know what you want to create, and explain the benefits they can expect *from* the group, as well what they will be expected to give *to* the group. When members know what is expected, you increase the odds that the group will survive.

It's a good idea to start small with six people at most. This provides an opportunity for prospective members to discuss their expectations from the group and what they can give. It also allows you to find a mutually convenient meeting time, which isn't easy to do with six, let alone a larger group.

There are seven keys to making a Peer Group work for all members:

1. **Participants must be willing to *give* as well as *get*.** Far too many groups fail because some members are just there to get and don't provide the same amount of help to other members. If each member gives time and undivided attention to others, the group will grow stronger.

2. **Be honest**. Let's face it, no one really *likes* to hear that their story needs improvement or just isn't working. But if they truly want to improve, they'll listen. If another member's story is confusing or doesn't connect with you, say so. Be respectful and specific. It isn't enough to say it isn't working; you need to provide reasons why and give detailed ideas to improve the story. Most people struggle with this step. They're afraid that if they get too specific, they'll hurt the other person's feelings. If you have trouble giving honest feedback, ask yourself

this question before you speak: "Would I benefit and improve if someone gave me the advice I'm about to give?"

3. **Have a thick skin.** As mentioned in the last point, receiving feedback isn't always fun. It isn't meant to be. But if you want to improve, constructive evaluation is necessary. Before committing to this type of group, carefully consider this question: "Am I doing this for education or validation?" If it's the latter, don't bother joining. Education leads to expansion; validation leads to stagnation.

4. **Respect other people's time.** As obvious as this may seem, it is violated far too often. If one member consistently takes up most of the meeting time, it will cause frustration and, eventually, fracture the group. Set a time limit for each person to speak and be evaluated. You can always make exceptions if someone needs special attention.

5. **Record yourself.** Providing the group with a recorded version of your story can help them assist you even more. They will get more insight into your style and effectiveness from hearing how you perform live with pauses and audience reactions.

6. **Write out your story.** Give the group a written copy of your presentation. This can help them offer suggestions about sentence structure, word usage, and overall flow of the story. Remember that some words and phrases may look good on paper but don't sound good to the ear. Writing your story does take time, but it's well worth that time because it offers another level of evaluation.

7. **Crave feedback.** This is the most important characteristic to bring to your group. If you truly seek improvement and are willing to help others, you will grow faster than you can imagine. The most successful people tend to be voracious students. They can never get enough knowledge or improve fast enough. Adopt this attitude and you, too, can rise above the pack.

In a fast-changing world, it's easy to get caught up in fads and trends, but principles of success work regardless of the latest trends. The concept of the Mastermind has existed for decades, if not centuries. Follow the rules laid out above, find a group of like-minded people, and commit to it. You'll find that the power of many minds can steer you to much greater heights.

**ACTION STEP:** Take your first steps to create a Mastermind of presenters and storytellers. Reach out to like-minded people. Use the seven steps in this lesson to create a foundation for your group.

**RECOMMENDED RESOURCE:** The classic book by Napoleon Hill, *Think and Grow Rich.* Pay close attention to Chapter 10, "Power of the Mastermind: The Driving Force." This chapter offers greater detail into how to create a powerful mastermind group. To get your copy, click here: http://amzn.to/1BVDPwS.

# Step 11 - Storytelling Lessons from the First Knight

I recently watched the movie, "First Knight." One of the key characters, Lancelot (played by Richard Gere), is a skilled swordsman who travels from town to town, dueling all challengers in sword fights to win money. Everywhere he goes, he wins these battles.

At one stop, a townsman asks, "Lancelot, will you teach me your secrets so I can be like you?"

Lancelot replies, "Do you really want to know my secrets, my good man?"

"I do. I'll do whatever it takes."

"There are 3 keys to winning:

1. **Know your opponent.**
2. **Fight with confidence.**
3. **Have no concern as to whether you live or die.**"

With that, the townsman turned and walked away.

So, what does this have to do with storytelling? More than you might think. Lancelot's three keys to winning parallel keys to presenting before an audience:

**1) Know your audience.** Far too often, speakers walk into presentations not knowing anything about the people who will hear them. Whether you're in a one-on-one sales situation, you're a keynote speaker or a trainer, if you know something about your audience, you dramatically increase your odds of connecting and providing points that last long beyond your presentation.

Additionally, just like in sword fighting, if you know where your audience might "strike," you can be prepared. You'll be ready if they disagree with you and challenge you. For example, if you're a financial advisor telling a story about a deceased client whose family was saved because she owned life insurance, you may get people who say that you're just using that story to manipulate their emotions or that your client's story is unusual and unlikely to happen to them. Having responses prepared beforehand will help you deal with those types of encounters.

**2) Speak with confidence.** Much like the swordsman, when you show confidence, you let the audience know that you believe in what you're doing and that you can accomplish what you came to do.

How do you build confidence? Only speak about subjects for which you have great passion. Know your material. Offer a message that focuses on the benefits to the audience.

Then, it's time to prepare. Practice. Rehearse. Get feedback. And then make adjustments. The more you internalize your message, the easier it will be to pivot when you're asked an unexpected question, when the meeting planner changes the length of your presentation, or when your audience simply isn't responding to you. Preparation builds confidence.

**3) Be willing to "die," i.e. fail.** In a recent lesson, you were reminded that with one exception, no one has ever died from giving a speech. When you're giving a story, you don't have to go quite as far as Lancelot's admonition to "not care whether you live or die." However, if you're willing to stand before an audience and not care about the outcome, you can make a deep connection.

What does this mean? Many presenters have an agenda. Perhaps it's to win a contract with a prospective client, to win a speech contest, or to persuade people to their way of thinking about a controversial subject. In each of these cases, there is an element of competition. The client might not sign the contract, the judges might not award the speaker the winning trophy, or the audience might not change their minds about the controversial subject. If this happens, speakers often feel as if they've "lost." Theirs ego are too focused on the outcome.

What if you give your presentation or share your story with the mindset that *you can't lose what you don't have?* In the examples above, the presenter never had the contract, the trophy, or the agreement of the audience. If she was able to achieve any of these three positive outcomes, she would've gained something. If not, she's no worse off than before she spoke.

Adopting this one change of mindset can dramatically improve your impact on an audience. They sense that you're there to share a message and not worried about an outcome. They'll be more relaxed because they'll feel your sincerity and believe that you have their best interest at heart.

You're not involved in a duel every time you stand before an audience. They want you to succeed and give them something of value. Adopt the three keys of Lancelot, and your message will resonate deeply.

**ACTION STEP:** Implement the three keys of the First Knight. Research your audience before you speak. Prepare and practice your presentation.

Adopt the mindset that you can't lose what you don't have. You're offering the audience a gift, which is your message. If they accept it, that's great! If not, you have lost nothing.

**RECOMMENDED RESOURCE:** The book, *Crucial Conversations: Tools for Talking When Stakes are High.* Although these aren't writings about storytelling or speaking, this book offers great insight into improving interpersonal conversations when there are important issues on the line. I've picked up tools from these authors that helped improve my presentation skills. To get your copy visit: http://amzn.to/ZVZgR3.

# Part 2

# How to Develop *Stand OUT!* Stories

# Step 12 - **Without a Skeleton, the Body Can't Stand**

Imagine a person without a skeleton. How easy would it be for her to stand up? Sit down? Lie down? Isn't it more likely that she would be a blob on the floor? Without a strong skeleton or structure upon which to build a body, human beings couldn't live to their full potential. They couldn't survive. The same is true of stories.

If you want to create a memorable story that resonates deeply, remember these words: **No structure equals no story.**

When most people write their presentations and their supporting stories, they try to think of a title, followed by their opening, theme, a couple of stories, and a conclusion. But that's like building a house by nailing some boards together, putting up some walls, then a roof, and just hoping it stays together.

Without first digging a hole in the ground, pouring a foundation, laying down a floor, and erecting solid beams to support the rest of the house, there is no home. It can't last.

The same is true of your stories. Without a logical framework to build them on, they will not be remembered, and there will be no impact on your audience.

Some presenters do something even worse when they develop their talks. They use that tool, the mere mention of which creates panic and horror in meeting rooms all across the world. You may have guessed it:

PowerPoint.

Many times, when I interview prospective clients for speech coaching, they say something like, "Well, Mike, I've created my PowerPoint; now, I need to fill in the speech."

This is wrong on so many levels:

1. The PowerPoint presentation is *not* your message.
2. It's imperative that your message and supporting materials be written first. Then, and only then, if appropriate, PowerPoint can be used to *supplement* your message.
3. No PowerPoint presentation will ever create the emotional connection and impact that a well-told, relevant story will create.

When these clients hire me, they do so with the understanding that the PowerPoint file will be set aside, the presentation and stories will be created upon a foundation, and then, if relevant, some slides may be brought back to support the key points.

This is the second dimension of the 3D Storytelling process—*Develop Your Story*.

Once they go through the process, they experience the power of properly structured stories. As a result, they have a much greater impact on their audiences.

The development of your story will begin with the creation of an overall theme. If you begin writing the story without connecting it to the overall theme of your presentation, you run into the problem that many storytellers face—the story doesn't resonate because it doesn't have a purpose. It only serves to confuse the audience.

This process, if properly used, will enable you to improve your impact, increase your number of prospective clients, and speed up your career growth.

In subsequent lessons, this development phase will be broken down into managcable pioces so that you can build one skill on another. In the next lesson, you'll learn a very important formula.

**ACTION STEP:** Pick a story from your story file, one in which someone experienced a change—you, a client in your business, a child you've impacted, or a coworker you've helped. Make sure it's a story where a product, service, or idea made a change in someone's life. You'll develop this in the coming weeks into one of your "signature stories."

**RECOMMENDED RESOURCE:** The book, *The Message of You,* by Judy Carter. Judy is a long-time standup comic and has instructed many people on the art of humor and comedy. She has a unique ability to touch the hearts of an audience, bringing them to tears one minute and hysterical laughter the next. This book will help you dig deep into your bank of stories and uncover the ones that will create deep bonds with an audience. To get your copy, visit: http://amzn.to/1r8kncM.

# Step 13 - **Then, Now, and How**

Remember my client, Patti, the self-confessed "rambler"? Whenever she gave a presentation, she would take much longer than necessary to communicate her ideas. Her talks were disjointed and left people feeling confused and frustrated. They just couldn't understand the purpose of her message.

Chances are, you've listened to a speaker who made you feel that way, too.

Patti was able to get over her rambling and have great success by using a process I learned from Darren LaCroix and Craig Valentine. It's called **Then, Now,** and **How.** Patti utilized this concept to develop a talk that was funny, inspirational, and touched lives. At the conclusion of her speech, she experienced three positive outcomes: a standing ovation, new donations of money to her foundation, and people volunteering their time to that same foundation.

The process enabled Patti to use the power of curiosity to capture and maintain audience interest.

Are you the least bit curious how Patti made her transformation? Wouldn't you like to know how she did it?

Before you learn the answers to those questions, though, think about your level of interest in Patti's story *right now*. Imagine what it would feel like for your audience to feel that same level of curiosity about your message each time you speak.

Patti delivered her speech with impact because she learned several *Stand OUT!*speaking tools, including:

1. *How to capture her audience with an Opening Bang.*
2. *How to use relevant stories that keep interest throughout her talk.*
3. *How to offer one Next step that compels the audience to take Action.*

These are the steps in the formula that helped her grab and keep audience interest from start-to-finish:

1. **THEN Step**: In this step, you introduce the circumstances of your character before she experienced a change. In Patti's case, she was feeling anxiety, fear, and sickness just at the *thought* of giving a speech. Obviously, those are not positive emotions. Those

THE Book on Storytelling

feelings connect with others because most people have experienced them about giving a speech.

An important part of this step is that *the worse the conditions, the better the story*. It doesn't get much worse than the feelings Patti experienced. Another key aspect of this step is to escalate the difficulty. As you may recall, Patti was looking at nearly a year of those feelings getting worse as the date of her speech approached.

2. **NOW step:** This is the step that highlights the improved circumstances of the character after experiencing the change. In Patti's case, she experienced the three positive outcomes described earlier. Those experiences generated positive feelings for her—the same feelings audience members want to feel.

3. **HOW step:** This is the step where you reveal the reason the change occurred. This could also be called the "Cure." These are lessons, processes, or tools that created the change. For Patti, this was learning *Stand OUT!* speaking tools like those mentioned earlier.

There are two keys aspects of this step if it's going to work to maximum effect. The first is that this part is about the lessons, processes, or tools that led to the cure. Most speakers make the mistake of bragging about themselves as the solution or source of the cure. Many speakers might say, "I taught Patti the *Stand OUT!* speaking processes and tools that she used" or "After working with me, Patti was able to get a standing ovation and donations of time and money to her foundation."

Are these statements true? Yes. Do they create a connection to the audience? Maybe not. Hearing someone brag about their own successes tends to turn people off. While it's true they want to know how someone solved a problem, they're more impressed by the solution than the person who provided it.

On the other hand, when you brag about the processes or tools, you increase the audience's desire to learn that same information. It just so happens that you are the person who can provide those solutions!

Remember this point: **People will trust and buy into a proven formula or process much faster than they'll buy into you.**

The second key aspect of the How step is the order in which the ideas are told. It must be *Then, Now, and How* for maximum effectiveness. Why? The order creates curiosity and suspense. For example, if the order was *Then, How, and Now*, you would first meet Patti and hear about her struggles. Then, you'd hear about the cure, or the processes and tools that she learned. Knowing the cure before hearing the end result, are you still going to be curious? Maybe. But you're probably going to guess the speech went well, so there's no suspense.

By knowing that her speech went well before you learn the cure, aren't you now curious to know how she was able to make such a drastic change? This is why the How step works best when it is presented last.

Telling a story that arouses curiosity and compels people to take action can be a major challenge. With a proven formula, you can connect with an audience and keep them on the edge of their seats until the end of your story. *Then, Now, and How* does just that.

**ACTION STEP:** Take the story that you selected after the last lesson, one in which someone experienced a change. Write down the emotions the person felt before the change occurred. Remember, the more intense or difficult the emotions, the better the story. Then, write down the emotions and the results experienced after the change. Finally, write out the solution(s) that inspired that change, i.e. whether it's a product, an idea, concept, or some other solution. This exercise will be the foundation of your *Then, Now, and How* story.

**RECOMMENDED RESOURCE:** The book, *World Class Speaking*, by Craig Valentine and Mitch Meyerson. This book teaches world class speaking and storytelling concepts, as well as ideas about building a successful speaking business. Craig and Mitch have provided me with many foundational ideas that transformed my business and lifted my speaking and storytelling skills to a new level. To get your copy, visit: http://amzn.to/1pzbZh1.

# Step 14 - Let Your Lighthouse Guide Your Story

Picture a lighthouse on the coast of Maine, solidly built on the rocky coastline and standing up to the pounding waves of the Atlantic Ocean. What is the purpose of that structure? It's a beacon that tells ships if they're off course.

Have you ever heard a story go off course? Have you ever *told* a story that went off course? Anyone who has ever presented is guilty of this at some point and needed help to get a story back on track.

Wouldn't it be great if your story could have a lighthouse? What if that lighthouse was available before you ever speak to a live audience?

Actually, that kind of beacon does exist. It's called a "Foundational Phrase." It's the stick by which every part of a presentation or story is measured. It will help you create a message that resonates with your audience and help them remember it long after you finish speaking.

**Every part of your story should be measured against the Foundational Phrase to determine if it belongs in your story.**

Consider some of these Foundational Phrases:

*Stand Up, Stand OUT!*
*Trust the Car!*
*Coke is IT!*

What do these have in common (aside from the exclamation point at the end of each)? They are short. They are declarative. They stir emotions.

The first two are programs that I've created. The third was created by a small bottling company you may have heard of that's based in Atlanta, Georgia.

The messages should be short because the fewer the words, the more likely they will be remembered. The words should be emotional because those are the type of phrases that connect with people. And the message must be clear. Otherwise, the audience will just walk away confused, and your story will quickly be forgotten.

Ask me how I know this!

My program *Stand Up, Stand OUT!* focuses on how to create and deliver meaningful and memorable messages. The early version of this program had a slightly longer title: "*Create a Meaningful and Memorable Message, and Deliver it in a Dynamic Style so that People Remember*

*You Long After You Speak, and You'll be Invited Back Time and Time Again."*

You think that's just a tad bit long? There is no way you could remember that title three seconds after hearing it, much less three days, three weeks, or three months later. But just like building a lighthouse from the foundation up, it was a starting point. After repeated testing and cutting, further testing and cutting, more testing and more cutting, the original 31-word title was whittled down to its final version: *Stand Up, Stand OUT!*

At their core, both titles say the same thing. The shorter version is simply easier to remember. When it's easier to remember, people are more likely to use it and share it.

If you're not convinced of the power of a short Foundational Phrase, try this little test. If you were born before 1965, you'll probably pass. If you were born in 1965 or after, you'll probably fail. But that's OK. Keep reading! There's a valuable lesson here for you, too!

Here's the test: Fill in the second half of this phrase:

**"Winston Tastes Good** _____

_____.**"**

What words popped into your head? If you're familiar with those first three words, the phrase "like a cigarette should" immediately popped into your mind. "Winston Tastes Good Like a Cigarette Should" was a popular advertising slogan for 18 years. Here's the twist: As of this writing in 2014, that ad hasn't run for *43 years*! Yet, if you were alive then, the words immediately popped into your brain. That's the power of a strong Foundational Phrase.

So, why is your Foundational Phrase important? For your story to have long-lasting impact, it must be wrapped around a foundational message. Remember, it's easy to get caught up in a story because you like it. Avoid the fate of other presenters who are adrift, telling stories without a beacon to guide their way. Use the Foundational Phrase to ensure that your story supports the message you want your audience to take away.

**ACTION STEP:** Create the first version of your Foundational Phrase. It should center around the main message you want your audience to walk away with. Don't edit; simply write down the emotional impact you want to create. Then, go out and test your phrase. Analyze your feedback. Test it again. Make adjustments. Test it again. Eventually, you will find your Foundational Phrase.

**RECOMMENDED RESOURCE:** The book, *So What,* by Mark Magnacca. Mark is a master of boiling down your message to its essence. He even includes an exercise that will help you quickly tell others what you do in a networking group, for example. This message will compel them to say "Really? Tell me more." To get your copy, visit: http://amzn.to/Wuwrc5.

# Step 15 - **Drop a Rock on Your Audience**

Imagine that you're standing next to a large pond. You pick up a huge rock and drop it in. What happens to the rock? There's a large splash. Large ripples are created. The rock sinks right to the bottom.

Now, imagine that you're standing next to that same pond. You pick up a small, flat stone and toss it across the surface. If you do it right, what should happen? Skip, skip, skip, skip to the other side. There are tiny ripples at the points where the stone contacts the water. There is no splash.

That pond represents the minds (the pond surface) and hearts (the pond bottom) of your audience. Most speakers present so many ideas to an audience that it's akin to tossing a bunch of stones across the pond surface. They "skip" right over the minds of the audience, and nothing sinks in.

The best speakers focus on one or two ideas and tell them in such a manner that they penetrate the minds and sink into the hearts of the audience.

Let's say you're sitting in an auditorium waiting to hear about a subject you're really interested in. A speaker stands at the front of the room and proceeds to bombard you with a plethora of information. At one point, you wonder if the speaker is going to take a breath! When the presentation ends, you feel tense, your head hurts, and you can't remember a word you just heard.

Have you ever had that experience? The person threw everything he had at you. Too much information.

In an attempt to share as much as possible, most speakers "skip" a lot of ideas and concepts at their audience. The audience loses interest and becomes confused.

People also have little, if any, time for reflection when you present too many ideas. Inspiring ideas or interesting concepts are useless if audience members don't have time to consider how those ideas could help them. Your story just becomes a lot of background noise, and you get tuned out.

This occurred to me with one of my stories called "Cornfield Wisdom." The central theme of the speech is that you should keep an open mind to new and unexpected opportunities. The main story reveals how I learned this lesson when I asked my girlfriend, Linda, to marry me while we were standing in a cornfield.

It's important to note that it wasn't my intention to get engaged in a cornfield. My very carefully laid out plans for the whole day had fallen apart, and it was almost out of desperation that I asked Linda in that cornfield.

Her response was, "Of course, I'll marry you, Michael." But that didn't change the fact that I felt bad to the point of embarrassment that I had proposed to her in a cornfield. When I told her that, she said, "Michael, you don't understand. I love cornfields. I love spontaneity. I love *you*. It was the *perfect* proposal." That's when I was reminded of the importance of being open to new and unexpected opportunities.

This story resonates with audiences and helps them also open up to new ideas and opportunities. However, in the original version, the story didn't resonate. That's because I had added a twist to the story.

Originally, I talked about being painfully shy and afraid of girls in high school, so much so that I never said two words to a girl I had a *huge* crush on in my junior year. After high school, I lost touch with her. We went our separate ways and led our lives.

Fast forward 30 years. Due to the magic of Facebook, I was able to track that girl down. We became long-distance friends, and she eventually moved back to our hometown. We became even better friends, so much so that she was the woman in the cornfield who said "Of course, I'll marry you, Michael."

I *love* that twist to the story. And it is all true. Many of my audience members loved it, too. However, I consistently received feedback from them that the twist was confusing. They weren't sure how that related to being open to new opportunities or whether I was saying they should be patient or ... they just weren't sure what the message was.

I tried to move this story into different parts of the speech. I tried *anything* to make it work, but I kept getting the same feedback.

Reluctantly, with a heavy heart and a tear in my eye, I cut that part out of my story. It still pains me because I love that twist. But I have to practice what I preach. My story and my message are not for me; they're for the audience. It's my job to be crystal clear on that message. To paraphrase the late attorney Johnny Cochran, ***"If the story doesn't fit, you must omit."***

Fortunately, there is a small group of speakers who are masters of presenting just one or two ideas and building their entire presentation around those concepts. There is depth to their message, and it sinks into the hearts of their audience members, much like that large rock splashing and sinking deeply into the pond. The end result is an emotional connection that opens up the audience to a new ways of thinking, feeling, or acting. Remember, that is the objective of any speech.

As you prepare your story, keep this concept in mind. Resist the temptation to give your audience everything you know. Give them one or two key ideas, and they'll be better off than they were before they heard you. This can only happen if you stop skipping stones over their heads and start dropping rocks into their hearts.

**ACTION STEP:** Present the first draft of your story to friends, family, or a Toastmasters club. Ask them to answer just one question: "Is this story and my message clear, or are there too many points? Is it confusing?" Make sure you are sharing no more than one or two key ideas.

**RECOMMENDED RESOURCE:** The audio program, *Mastering Your Speech*, by Lance Miller. You were introduced to Lance in Step 6. He helped take my speaking to a much higher level when he convinced me to focus on my speech evaluation skills. Lance has a unique perspective on speaking, and this program can give you new skills to take your current ones to a higher level. To get your

copy, visit:
http://www.lancemillerspeaks.com/products.php.

# Step 16 - **Convince Them to Stay**

Have you ever listened to a speaker and wondered "Why am I listening to this guy?" or "That's 30 minutes I'll never get back."

More importantly, have *you* ever given a presentation where audience members asked those same questions? You haven't? So, you're the one! Unfortunately, the rest of us have had that experience.

Is there a way to eliminate those questions in the minds of your audience? Yes! It's called your Big Promise.

This is one sentence that you deliver near the beginning of your presentation. It tells the audience exactly what they will receive from your talk. If you want your stories to have maximum impact, they must relate to your Big Promise. Otherwise, the audience will become confused about your purpose.

Consider this example from our 3D Storytelling program:

*What if you had a process to create messages that leave a lasting impact on your audience?* **The 3D Storytelling process will provide you with 3 tools** *to create meaningful and memorable messages.* *With these, you can create stories that help you Stand Out every time you Stand Up before an audience.*

Do you see how the Big Promise tells the audience exactly what they'll receive and the benefits they'll walk away with? Most speakers don't give this gift to their audience. They leave people in the dark, guessing what they're going to get for investing their valuable time and attention.

The way you phrase your Big Promise is also important. Many speakers make the mistake of sounding something like this:

*"Today, I'd like to tell you about our program, 3D Storytelling. I'm going to tell you the three steps, and then, I'll tell you how this program helped me create more meaningful messages."*

Did you hear that? "I" this and "me" that. Who is the focus in those statements? The speaker, not the audience. And who really cares about the speaker? You're right—nobody except the speaker and his/her mom.

At a subconscious level, people in the audience are thinking "I don't care what you'd like" or "I don't care what you want. What I'm here for is ME!"

Compare the "I-focused" statement with the way the statement was phrased earlier:

*What if **you** had a process to create messages that leave a lasting impact on **your** audience? The 3D Storytelling process will provide **you** with 3 tools to create meaningful and memorable messages. With these, **you** can create stories that help **you** Stand Out every time **you** Stand Up before an audience.*

That's six *you's* or *yours* and no *I's* or *me's*. Who is the focus now? The audience. Where is the focus supposed to be? The audience. Are they more likely to listen to you now? Absolutely.

This is a subtle but very important difference. Craig Valentine calls this a "slight edge" principle. Structuring your Promise around "you" versus "I" makes the audience members feel as if you're talking to them individually rather than as a group. That slight edge equals a huge difference.

You can avoid falling into the trap of talking about yourself or leaving your audience guessing what your speech is about. Create your Big Promise, and your audience will no longer think "Why should I listen to you?" Instead, they'll think, "Tell me more!"

**ACTION STEP:** Create your Big Promise. Tell your audience exactly what they'll receive, as well as the ultimate benefit. Be specific about this benefit, and make sure that promise is "you" focused, rather than "I" focused.

**RECOMMENDED RESOURCE:** The audio program called "Create Your Keynote By Next Week." It was developed by Darren LaCroix and Patricia Fripp. Even if your goal is not to develop keynote speeches, I highly suggest this program. Darren interviews Ms. Fripp and gathers nearly 40 years of speaking nuggets in one program. It offers a step-by-step process to develop speeches and stories, and it will save you a tremendous amount of time. To get your copy, visit: http://www.profcs.com/app/?af=750771. Click the *Improve Public Speaking* tab from the Online Store. In the section called "How to Write a Speech," click the "Create Your Keynote by Next Week" tab.

# Step 17 - Curiosity Killed the Cat But Keeps Audiences Alive

If you've seen one of the popular CSI-type shows, how do they typically open? A dead body is found by an unsuspecting passerby. You immediately start asking questions: "Who is that person?" "How did she die?" "Who killed her?"

These shows are terrific at creating curiosity. During the ensuing 60 minutes, your questions are answered as the mystery unfolds, and the killer or killers are revealed.

What keeps your attention through the program? Not knowing who did the deed. If the killer was revealed in the opening, you might still watch, but only because you had nothing better to do. There would be no suspense or tension.

You no doubt know the old adage, "Curiosity killed the cat." I'm not sure why it killed the cat, but I do know that without curiosity, your story will die. Your audience needs compelling reasons to listen to your story through to its conclusion.

The best way to generate curiosity is to create questions in the minds of the audience. This will keep their interest. Waiting for the answers to those questions is the ultimate payoff for them, which is why they will stay to the end.

The best place to create questions is in your opening. Although there are many ways to open your speech, three of the most effective are:

1. Jump right into your story.
2. Recite a quote.
3. Ask a direct question.

Some speakers love to jump right into their stories. You can describe an interesting scene, make a startling statement, or describe a character to grab attention and arouse curiosity.

For example, "Judy walked into my office, slumped into the chair next to my desk, and sat quietly, staring out of the window. You could tell that she had been crying, and there were dark circles under her eyes. She looked unkempt, and seemed as if she had aged 10 years in the last four weeks."

Has this scene piqued your interest? Why was Judy crying? Why did she look so bad? What happened four weeks ago?

These types of questions will sustain people's attention because you've aroused their curiosity.

The second tool - using a quote - is a different approach. Quotes are useful if they set up your story. In my program, *Ignite Your Passion, Take ACTION!*, I sometimes open with this quote "The late speaker, Jim Rohn, once said, 'The pain of action weighs ounces compared to the pain of regret, which weighs tons.'" [xiv] This quote creates questions about regret and action, and it orients the audience to the upcoming material. They're curious to see where the speech is going and how it can help them.

When using quotes, be sure that they relate specifically to your topic. Many speakers fall into a trap of using quotes because they sound good, not because they support the main point of the speech. Unrelated quotes can confuse and even irritate audiences when they don't add to your message. Darren LaCroix once made this suggestion to me: "Don't use a quote unless it has specifically had an impact and made a change in your life." This is excellent advice.

The third tool, questions, can create immediate involvement for the listener. For example, a financial advisor could ask an audience, "If you had to retire today, how long would your money last?" or "If you did not make it home tonight, how long could your family maintain their lifestyle?" Don't these questions engage you on an emotional level? Would you like to at least hear some ideas to help answer those questions? In just two sentences, you're involved in the speech.

Asking questions can create an emotional connection with your audience and keep their interest throughout your presentation. Keep an important point in mind, though: As critical as it is to create curiosity, it's equally important to answer those questions. Unanswered questions in a speech leave the audience feeling unfulfilled, confused, and even annoyed. Create curiosity, but also make sure you satisfy that curiosity before you walk away.

Curiosity may have killed the cat, but *not* creating curiosity can kill your story. To involve your audience, create questions in their minds. Pique their interest, and you will have their attention from start to finish.

**ACTION STEP:** Review your story to determine if you're creating curiosity. Do your stories and quotes create questions that grab the audience's attention? Are you spurring questions early in the presentation? Then, are you answering all of the questions by the end of your story?

**RECOMMENDED RESOURCE:** The book *Resonate*, by Nancy Duarte. This is one of the best books I've read about the art of storytelling. Ms. Duarte explores the storytelling arc and explains, in straightforward and common sense language, why stories work and how you can craft memorable stories that resonate deeply with audiences. To get your copy, visit: http://amzn.to/1vC4Ntv

# Step 18 - **Break the Rules**

Before we leave the subject of curiosity, let's discuss an issue that often comes up in speaking—rules about how to structure your speech and deliver it.

There are some essential rules you should always follow:

1. **Respect your audience's time**. If you violate this, you'll lose their attention and your credibility.
2. **Don't insult your audience** or the people who hire you. This one is pretty obvious.
3. **Do not use the platform simply to sell your product or services**. Be a content-rich speaker. Speakers who do nothing but sell their products or services anger both the audience and the meeting planner, and they almost never get asked back.

Besides these rules, however, there are long-held beliefs in the speaking world that can limit your presentations. Generally, there's no right or wrong way to create and deliver a presentation. As Patricia Fripp says, you have theatrical choices that can make your presentations more effective.

For example, one "rule" that has been passed down for decades is the idea that when you present your speech, you should *Tell 'em what you're going to tell them. Tell 'em. Then, tell 'em what you just told 'em.*

On the surface, this sounds like good advice. Done properly, it can be effective and sell your message. Unfortunately, most speakers give away the ending and kill curiosity before they get to their stories.

Is this a *wrong* choice? No, but if that's what everyone else is doing and the audience isn't curious, how will you and your message stand out?

Take the movie, "Titanic," for example. As you walked into the theater, you knew one thing for sure—that boat was going down. No question there. So, why did you sit down for 3 hours and 20 minutes? Director James Cameron kept you curious until the conclusion.

How would you have felt in the first 10 minutes if elderly Rose, the heroine, had listed the names of all of her friends and family who died in the disaster? You may have still watched the movie for the special effects, but there would have been no intrigue or compelling reason to be emotionally involved with the movie.

By introducing each of the key characters and telling their stories, Cameron builds suspense in his film. The tension and curiosity continues to build after the Titanic hits the iceberg, the water level continues to rise, and each of the character's fates is eventually revealed.

If Cameron had followed the mantra of *Tell 'em what you're going to tell 'em. Tell 'em. Then, tell 'em what you told 'em,* you would have known everyone's fate at the beginning, and all curiosity would have been lost. I doubt that "Titanic" would have earned a billion dollars if he had followed this rule.

To respect your audience and keep their interest, there are some hard-and-fast rules you should follow, but some rules also need to be broken if your message is going to have long-term benefits for your audience. When you take the risk to be different and break a couple of them, you increase your odds of standing out from the crowd.

**ACTION STEP:** Share your story with others to determine if you're giving away too much information early in your presentation. Ask them specifically if they felt curious early on and if you answered that curiosity by the end of your story. Watch movies like "Titanic" to learn how other storytellers tease audiences and build suspense.

**RECOMMENDED RESOURCE:** Watch the video on YouTube of Steve Jobs introducing the iPhone. No one created curiosity better than Jobs. As a speaker, he was a master of the dramatic, and his legendary presentations helped make Apple a household name. From his style of dress in the workplace to his use of visuals in his talks to the products he imagined and helped create, Jobs helped rewrite the way we do business and the way we live. Watch this video, and see a man who could wow his audience with curiosity and by being different:

https://www.youtube.com/watch?v=x7qPAY9JqE4
.

# Step 19 - **The Devil is in the Details**

One key to attracting audience attention early in a story is to describe circumstances. A good way to do this is to provide details, either about the characters, the setting, or the interaction between characters.

This is a challenge for many presenters. They're either too vague, or they provide too much detail. Why is this a problem? If you're being too vague, the audience won't become emotionally involved with your story. It feels more like a short report instead of an experience. If there are too many details, the audience gets bogged down and, ultimately, bored.

For example, if director Victor Fleming had rushed through "The Wizard of Oz" movie, giving just a few details, Dorothy would have hit her head, woke up in a castle, seen quite a few strange creatures around her, caught a glimpse of a straw guy on fire, tossed water on him, and melted some nasty-looking green woman. There wouldn't have been any tension or suspense, and the audience probably wouldn't have cared because there was no time to build an emotional bridge to the characters in the story.

On the other hand, if Mr. Fleming had taken 35 minutes to show every detail of the cyclone skirting across the Kansas landscape, hitting the house, picking it up into the air, soaring for many miles, and eventually landing in Oz, audiences would have gotten bored and emotionally checked out.

There's a fine line between capturing the audience's attention and elevating the suspense without overloading them with details. Remember, you're not writing a novel; you're creating a story to support a message.

The key is to tease them with just enough information and let them fill in the rest. For instance, in my speech, "Cornfield Wisdom," I describe the scene where I got engaged in a cornfield:

*"The hot August sun beat down on me. The sweat was beading on my upper lip. With the smell of a nearby chicken coop hanging in the air, I looked into her beautiful hazel eyes and pulled out a ring box. 'Honey, this day hasn't gone at all like I planned. But there's something I've been wanting to ask you all day. Will you marry me?'"*

Here are three questions for you about that story:

1. What was the temperature that day?
2. How far away was the chicken coop?
3. What is the size of the ring?

Your initial reaction might be, "Michael, how should I know? You didn't describe them." Actually, you do know. The details were intentionally designed to flavor the scene but allow you to participate in creating it.

Are you confused? Here's what I mean. Take, for example, the phrase *"hot August sun beat down..."* That tells you it was a hot day. *You* get to fill in the minor details. One person may picture a 100-degree day with a cloudless sky; another might see an 85-degree, humid, overcast day. Those details are not critical to the story and the main point it supports. The information is just vague enough to allow each audience member to fill in the details with his/her perception of "hot," and that helps them feel as if they're helping to create the story.

The same is true for the chicken coop and the size of the ring (which, by the way, my fiancée thinks is a large enough rock, thank you very much!). If I gave you every minute detail, you'd get bored, and I'd be cheating you out of participating in creating the scene. I'd also be cheating myself out of the opportunity to develop a deeper connection with you, the audience.

Keep this key point in mind: ***People buy into what they help create.*** As you develop your story, don't make the mistake many speakers do of either giving too few or too many details. Give your audience enough to flavor your scenes, and allow them to fill in the blanks. When they help create the story, it's no longer just your story; it's theirs, too.

**ACTION STEP:** Share your story with others, asking them if the amount of detail is too much, causing the pace to be slowed down. If not, ask if the amount of detail is too little, not developing enough interest in it. Audio or video record your speech and play back the recording. If you were an audience member, would you feel that you were given the opportunity to participate in creating this story, or would you feel that the story is bogged down with too many details, causing you to lose interest?

**RECOMMENDED RESOURCE:** The book, *Storytelling for Financial Advisors,* by Scott West and Mitch Anthony. Don't let the title fool you. This isn't a book just for financial professionals. There are excellent examples of how to appeal to the emotional side of your audience, how to use metaphors, and how to replace statistics with memorable stories. I've used the concepts in this book for years with great success. To get your copy, visit: http://amzn.to/1uzaJ3a.

# Step 20 - Help Your Audience Come to Their Senses

Consider the difference between these two versions of the same scene:

Version One: *"I'll never forget the holidays at my grandparents' house. The place was always festive. The family would gather there, and we would have a great time together. Aside from opening presents, eating grandma's home-cooked meals was the best part of the day."*

Version Two: *"How well do you remember the holidays with your family? Christmas at my grandparents' house will always stay with me. A 10-foot high, brightly decorated tree stood in the corner of the living room. You could smell pine scent in every part of the house. You could hear the laughter of excited kids over the sound of "It's a Wonderful Life" playing on TV. Other than the joy of ripping the wrapping paper off of our presents that morning, the best part of the day was eating grandma's turkey, mashed potatoes, and homemade pie. The loving feeling of being with my family is still with me 40 years later."*

What's the difference? Version two uses a tool that helps describe the circumstances and helps the audience feel as if they are *in* your story. That tool is describing as many senses as possible throughout the speech.

If possible, use all five. Sight. Smell. Touch. Hearing. Taste. The more you can incorporate into your story, the more involved your audience will be.

In the first version of our scene, you see generic phrases like "looked festive," "great time together," "home-cooked meals." These don't give sufficient detail, and they exclude specific sensory connection. They also don't give depth to the emotion of the moment. It feels more like a report.

Version Two, on the other hand, offers descriptions that make you feel as if you're *in* the scene. Notice that all five senses were involved:

- Can you *see* the 10-foot high, brightly decorated tree?
- Can you *smell* the scent of pine?
- Can you *hear* the laughter of kids and the sound of "It's a Wonderful Life" on the TV?
- Can you *taste* the turkey, mashed potatoes, and pie?
- Can you *feel* the excitement of the kids as they rip the wrapping paper off of their presents?

Don't you feel you were actually in that scene, witnessing the event, as opposed to Version One? That is the power of adding sensory details to your story. It moves your tale from a simple *retelling* to a more involved *reliving*.

Don't forget the lesson from the last chapter, however, about not going overboard with your details. In version two above, you pictured a particular color of lights and decorations on the tree that were familiar to *you*. You heard the voices of children of a certain age. You heard specific scenes that you remember from "It's a Wonderful Life."

If I had said "The 10-foot high tree with white, twinkling lights and silver tinsel," it might have conflicted with your idea of how the tree should look. If I had said, *"Can you hear the voice of George Bailey coming from the TV?"* it could have created a conflict in your world if the first character you think about in "It's a Wonderful Life" is Clarence, the Guardian Angel. It's much better if you give a hint of the scene and let the audience fill in the blanks.

When you provide sensory details, you transform the scene into an experience so that your audience relives your story with you. This, in turn, develops a deeper connection with listeners. They are not only more open to hearing your message, but they are more likely to *act* on your recommendations.

**ACTION STEP:** Review your story for sensory details. Be aware of generic words that don't create images or feelings. Replace those terms with specific sensory words. To increase the emotional connection, include as many of the five senses as possible.

**RECOMMENDED RESOURCE:** The book, *Influence,* by Robert Cialdini. This isn't a book specifically about speaking or storytelling, but it does provide an in-depth study of the reasons people are influenced. It also offers insight into how and why people are "wired" to react to specific words and sentences. It can provide you with valuable ideas on word usage as you create your stories. Many consider this to be the definitive study on the subject of influence. To get your copy, visit: http://amzn.to/VXbSoW.

# Step 21 - Set the Stage with Context

One of the best ways to grab your audience's attention and keep it is to describe circumstances early in your story. This applies to the setting, the characters, and the situation. Author Paul Smith calls this "describing the context."[xv]

Unfortunately, many speakers immediately jump right into their story without explaining why the audience should care about it. You may be thinking, *"OK, why is this a problem?"*

If your audience doesn't know the reason or the potential benefits of the story, they may be confused or simply not care.

As Mr. Smith further points out, the most effective order of presenting is:

**1) Give the Context of Your Story**
**2) Describe the Action of the Characters**
**3) Explain the Result and the Changes**
**which Occur**[xvi]

Context provides the background and sets the stage for the action that follows.

Consider the following premise: In my financial planning practice, we used to conduct a workshop called "Wine, Women, and Wealth." It was a women-only program. During the first two events, I didn't feel a connection with the audience. It felt like the attendees weren't fully engaged, maybe even suspicious of my intentions.

At the end of the second event, I gathered my courage and said, "Ladies, I believe in complete candor when I give a presentation. I can't shake this feeling that something is wrong. Would you mind telling me if I'm right?"

After a few seconds of silence, I thought, "Uh oh, maybe that was a serious mistake."

That's when a woman named Leslie said, "Mike, I like all the things you've said about managing my money. But I'm wondering, what's your angle?"

"I'm sorry, Leslie, my angle? I don't know what you mean."

"Look, you're one man talking to a room full of women, and you're buying us dinner and wine. I've been burned by these kinds of programs before. Do you have some kind of agenda, some other reason for doing this event?"

Other women nodded their heads in agreement.

For the first time, I stood back and saw the big picture. Our company was devoted to providing better financial education to women. But my male-focused brain hadn't considered that the wine and dinner aspect might look a little suspicious unless I gave a valid reason (or context) for providing financial education to women.

Here's what I said: "Leslie, thank you for saying that. I believe I understand your concerns. Here is why I do this program. When I was 25 years old, I happened to stop by my mom's house one day. I walked into her kitchen, and she was seated at the dining room table with a stack of bills and her open checkbook lying in front of her. She had tears in her eyes, which isn't normally like her. 'Mom, why are you crying?' I asked.

'I can't get any money, Michael!'

'What are you talking about? You've got a job, and you've got money in the bank.'

She said, 'That's not what I mean. I can't get a credit card or a loan.'

'That doesn't make any sense, Mom! You've always paid your bills on time. You've got a great credit rating.'

She stopped me. 'Everything was in your Dad's name. I paid the bills, but he got all the credit. When he moved out, he took the credit rating with him.

It's like I don't even exist....'

I hold these events to help other women avoid the pain I saw my mom go through that day."

For a few seconds, no one said a word, but you could feel the attitude shift in the room. I could see on their faces that they sensed my sincerity, and they trusted that I was there to help them.

That experience taught me a valuable lesson. Without the proper context, an audience can be confused or even misunderstand your intentions. The honesty of the women at that event helped me see the importance of providing context to your story. I still appreciate Leslie's candor and willingness to tell me how she felt.

Since that night, I've told every woman-only audience about that encounter with my mom. It has helped me build an immediate bond, develop trust, and quickly engage them in my presentations.

If you want to maximize the power of your story, give your audience the context before you dive into the action.

**ACTION STEP:** Review your presentation to determine if you're introducing the action too soon without providing context. Share your story with others, and ask them if you set up the importance of your story before you got into the details.

**RECOMMENDED RESOURCE:** The movie "Comedian." As you develop your story, you may occasionally feel frustrated as you try to improve it. "Comedian" follows Jerry Seinfeld after his legendary TV show left the air. It documents his frustrations as he attempted to develop new material in his return to the world of standup comedy.

Keep in mind that this is a man who was one of the most powerful individuals in show business at the time—at the top of the entertainment world—and he is shown experiencing the same feelings that you and I feel as we struggle to improve our stories.

BE WARNED: This film includes a lot of adult humor and language. If you're sensitive to that type of material, avoid this movie. To get your copy, visit: http://amzn.to/1tPBbsi.

# Step 22 - Bring Your Story to Life with Characters

Of all the components in your story, your characters are among the most important. Why? Because characters are what your audience will relate to.

In previous chapters, you learned about the concept of re*living* versus re*telling*. When you simply give a memorized talk, it feels as if you're re-telling your story, or giving a report. When you tell events through your characters—their dialogue, actions, and reactions—the audience gets to re-*live* your story. This is how you create a memorable experience.

As you develop your characters, it's important that people can relate to them. Craig Valentine once told me, "If the listener doesn't *know* your characters, they will not *care* about them. In order for them to relate, they must See, Know and Hear the characters."

At first glance, this may seem like a huge undertaking. The reality is, you can quickly give insight to your characters through short descriptions and dialogue. For example, for people to be *seen*, describe them in one or two sentences:

*Janice's gray hair and crow's feet gave a hint of her age, but her laughter and manner made her seem like a woman half that age.*

OR:

*Mark stood off to the side by himself with his head hanging down, but it was hard to miss him. He had long, dark, uncombed hair, and was a half-foot taller than every other kid in the room.*

What can you tell about these two characters? Janice is middle- or older-aged. She is probably a very optimistic person, has a good sense of humor, and most likely, has youthful energy. She is someone people like to be around.

Mark is probably a teenager, perhaps shy, as he's standing alone. He is not particularly fashionable or clean. He may feel awkward and different because of his height.

Are these all the details about your characters? No. But they're enough to give your audience a hint of what they look like.

After *seeing* the characters, your audience can *know* them through a quick back-story. *You* can do this, or you can allow other characters to do it through dialogue. For example:

*"Lisa, I can't believe it's been two years since John died."*

*"Dave, we still miss him so much, but we're moving on."*

Dave said, *"How did you feel when they convicted the other driver?"*

*"You know, not what I expected. I was... numb. Whatever they do to the guy, it's not gonna bring John back."*

*"Are Justin and Jason still in counseling?"*

Lisa said, *"Only occasionally. They're back into band and sports, and acting like teenagers again. They do talk to me and we cry together sometimes. I need the counseling more than they do."*

*"I understand, Lisa. The one good aspect of all this is that the life insurance allowed the three of you to not worry about money. You didn't have to go back to your practice until you were ready. From what your partners tell me, they were able to handle the patient load while you were away."*

*"Dave, they've been fabulous. I don't know how we would've gotten by without them. I know we're going to be OK."*

What do you know about Lisa? Through a conversation, you know that her husband John died two-years ago in a car accident caused by another driver. She has two teenage sons. They're all struggling with John's death but trying to move on. She is some type of medical professional. They are doing OK financially because of life insurance proceeds they received after the accident, and the support of her co-workers.

I could have said, "Lisa is a widowed mother of two teenage boys. Her husband John was killed in a car accident. She is a doctor, and although the family is struggling to move on, they are in good shape financially."

Doesn't quite have the emotional impact, does it? It's a short report. Delivered in dialogue between the characters, isn't Lisa more relatable, even sympathetic?

Your audience has now *seen* your characters, and *knows* some of their back story. To complete the picture, allow your characters to be heard.

You saw this in the last conversation. Lisa gave insight into her and her son's emotional states of mind. She also let you know that her sons are becoming active again and that her business associates have helped the family get through a difficult time.

As you previously learned, that's just enough detail to paint the picture—enough to let the audience fill in the rest. The information tells us about Lisa's current situation, how she got there, and her emotional state.

Characters are a key component to your story. Allow the audience to See, Know, and Hear your characters, and they will develop an emotional attachment to those characters. Your story will come to life, your audience will feel part of the story, and they will more likely remember your story and your message.

**ACTION STEP:** Develop ways for your characters to be Seen, Known and Heard. Create one or two sentences that describe each. Develop character dialogue that introduces back stories and offers insight into the personalities of your characters.

**RECOMMENDED RESOURCE:** The book, *Story Based Selling*, by Jeff Bloomfield. Although ostensibly written for salespeople, the concepts here are applicable to speaking as well. In a sense, speaking is simply selling from a stage to a larger group of prospective buyers. This book offers scientific insights into storytelling, as well as how

to dig deep to uncover your most powerful stories.
To get your copy, visit: http://amzn.to/1qjk2yT.

# Step 23 - **Struggles, Strife, and Setbacks**

One afternoon, after a heated family argument, I lost control. I stormed into my back yard. I picked up the first thing I saw - an aluminum baseball bat. I reached back, and with all my strength, I started whacking at everything in my path.

"I...CAN'T...TAKE...ANY...MORE...OF...THIS!!"

A few minutes later, when I started to come back to my senses, I realized I had just beaten the fence - my neighbor's fence. In that moment, I understood the term "blind rage."

That's when I saw him—my three-year-old son, Brenden. He had walked outside during my attack. He tentatively walked over toward me. He looked scared.

"Daddy, can I jump in the mud puddle?"

"What? You wanna do what? Jump in a puddle?"

Slowly, he nodded his head up and down.

"Look, I don't know, Brenden."

I looked into his big, brown, sad eyes. "Sure. Go ahead, Buddy."

He walked over to a puddle that had formed under his swing set after the previous night's downpour. Very gingerly at first, he stepped in. Then, he started jumping up and down, with much more gusto, until eventually he was covered with mud.

And that's when it hit me! He's relieving his stress. In the middle of all that chaos, he knew he had to do something to feel better.

It took my three-year-old son jumping in a mud puddle to make me realize I needed to find my own stress relievers.

This story is the centerpiece of my speech entitled, "Find Your Mud Puddles." If you're wondering why I'm telling you a story about me and my son getting muddy, the answer is this: By sharing my own embarrassment and pain and telling you about someone who helped me see life a little differently, I've hopefully made a connection with you.

Unfortunately, this is a process most speakers don't use because they're too busy building themselves up. Put another way, when you build yourself up, you also build a wall between you and your audience.

Why do so many speakers and presenters brag about themselves? Two reasons:

1. They feel it's necessary to build up their credibility.
2. They feel insecure or intimidated about presenting to an audience, so they feel they need to "look good."

What they don't realize is that when they do this, the audience typically thinks, "Oh, I could never do that. That guy is lucky or special." Worse, they might think "Who does she think she is? She's just up here bragging about herself. I'm not impressed by all this. I wanna know what she can do for me."

Either way, the outcome is not good.

Please don't misunderstand. The message here isn't "don't tell your audience about your successes.' At some point, they'll want to hear about your success so that you can give them hope. Before you do that, however, earn their trust. Let them know that you're just like them.

How do you do this? Share your struggles, strife, and setbacks. Everyone has experienced each of those situations. People not only relate to them, but hearing your story may help them feel just a little bit superior—and that's OK. *You're building your audience up.*

For instance, in my Mud Puddle story, I demonstrate how I acted like a fool and was irresponsible when I lost my temper. Audience members might think, "Well, I've lost it before, but not like that! Glad I'm not him... or his neighbor!"

This is the reaction you want. Now, they can relate to you, and they're open to hearing your message.

If you want to create that instant connection and bond, share your stories of struggle, strife, and setback before discussing your success. Do this, and people will not only feel like you, they will like you and want to hear more.

**ACTION STEP:** Review your story to make sure you're not just talking about your accomplishments. Be willing to talk about your difficulties. In fact, start your message talking about those struggles, and you'll gain the interest of your audience much more quickly.

**RECOMMENDED RESOURCE:** A short and entertaining video called "Find Your Puddle Today." This has nothing to do with my speech, but it's a reminder of the message to not only find your stress relievers, but enjoy the moment and the little opportunities that life presents to you. Visit http://bit.ly/10xAoPR to enjoy the video!

# Step 24 - **Conflict is the Hook**

In the "Star Wars" movie series, Darth Vader wreaked havoc on the galaxy. He was the prototypical bad guy. His son, Luke Skywalker, faced one obstacle after another until they had their epic showdown in the final movie.

The hook to this story was conflict. Through these movies, your interest is maintained because you know that eventually they will have to settle the score. A big reason you can relate to this is because you've experienced conflict in your own life.

Imagine, if early in the movie, upon learning that Vader was his father, Luke had thought, "Wow, that's a bummer, but, ehh, whatever. I'll just hang out at the farm, and maybe we'll run into each other from time to time."

Not very compelling, is it? Without conflict, your story is not worth telling. What types of conflict are there, and what kind should you consider?

There are four main types:

## 1) Person versus Environment
A person faces obstacles in his home, community, or area. One of the best examples is the story of the unnamed Chinese student who faced down tanks during the crackdown in Tiananmen Square in 1989. One person versus the military.

## 2) Person versus Nature
A person faces the danger of a natural disaster. For instance, a woman and her family do not evacuate their home in New Orleans in time to escape the onslaught of Hurricane Katrina. They face rising waters and the threat of being stranded until help arrives.

## 3) Person versus Person
Luke Skywalker versus Darth Vader. Batman versus the Joker. Superman versus Lex Luthor. These are great literary figures, to be sure. They're also excellent examples of one person in conflict with another .

## 4) **Person versus Him/Herself**

This is the most common and relatable of all conflicts. Movies and literature are filled with examples of this type: Dr. Jekyll and his alter-ego, Mr. Hyde; Captain Ahab from Moby Dick; Bruce Wayne and his alter ego, Batman. Each of these characters faced internal conflict, uncertainty, or doubt. Why are these stories so powerful? Because you can relate to inner conflict.

You're probably not facing a murderous monster fighting to come out of you, you aren't hunting a large whale, and you aren't deciding whether or not to be a masked vigilante. However, you do face internal struggles just like they did. Their solutions to their problems may give you insight into how your life can be better. Your story of overcoming conflicts and problems can help your audience in the same way.

Introducing the conflict is only the first step, however. There are two keys that maintain audience interest to the conclusion of your story.

One of them is to escalate the conflict. Think about a story you've heard that seemed long and boring. Chances are there was no relatable conflict or the pace of the conflict was either too slow or too fast, and you didn't get emotionally involved.

The pace at which you increase tension is critical. Picture an elevator or a moving walkway at an airport. If your story moves along at the pace of a moving walkway, with no increase in tension, the audience is going to lose interest.

No increase in tension = no rising conflict = no interest.

On the other hand, if your conflict escalates too quickly, your audience will miss it, and they won't feel a connection.

Referring back to the movie "Titanic," the initial conflicts occur within individual stories - Rose's reluctance to marry Cal and Jack's maneuvering to win his ticket onto Titanic. After Rose meets Jack, the conflicts increase - Rose wants to be with Jack, but her family is pressuring her to stay with Cal. Jack is falsely accused of theft and is handcuffed to a post, which later becomes a bit of a problem when the water gushes into the room in which he's being held.

After Titanic strikes the iceberg, the continual rising water triggers increasing tensions for each character. This continues until the conclusion of the film.

Once you've established a properly escalating conflict, the second key to maintaining interest is to resolve the conflict. Imagine reading a great novel or watching a movie in which you've connected with the characters. You've become emotionally involved in an escalating conflict and then, suddenly, the story ends without telling you how the conflict is resolved.

How would you feel? Irritated at the very least and maybe even angry. Don't leave your audience feeling that way. Just as we know that Luke Skywalker eventually won the battle and saved his father's soul, and Rose survived to live a long life, let your audience know how your story ends.

Conflict—it's the hook of great stories. Describe the inherent conflict, slowly increase it until it reaches a climax, and then explain the resolution. You'll then have a story that resonates with others and leaves them talking about you long after you speak.

**ACTION STEP:** Use at least one of the four types of conflicts in your story. Escalate the conflict at a steady pace until you reach the climactic moment. Then, give the audience the resolution of the situation and the impact on your character.

**RECOMMENDED RESOURCE:** A video from World Champion speaker Ed Tate called "How to Deal with Bullies." Ed is a highly successful professional speaker. This clip illustrates a terrific story with rising conflict and resolution. It offers a powerful message on how to deal with person-to-person conflict. Listen not only to the message, but watch a master speaker deliver in a powerful style. To watch the video, visit: http://bit.ly/ZZZOof.

# Step 25 - The Climax

You've introduced your characters. You've described the circumstances and increased the conflict. If you've properly built the tension, the audience is hooked. The story has escalated to its critical point.

Now, it's time to deliver the climax. This is the scene where the character(s) learn the lesson of your story and where they undergo a transformation. Hollywood screenwriting guru Michael Hague says that this change is necessary. The character cannot go back to the way life was. If there's no change, the audience will be let down.

What does the audience want to know at this point?

1. The lesson that was learned.
2. How the lesson changed the life of your characters.
3. How they can use it in their own lives.

In "A Christmas Carol," there is an obvious change in the character of Scrooge. In the beginning, he's a miserly and miserable old man. With the visit of each succeeding ghost, his internal tensions increase. It's only after the final visit from the Ghost of Christmas Future that he truly changes.

The lessons he learns, which the audience also takes away, are: Money alone will not make you happy and caring for others enriches your life. These lessons change Scrooge and make him a better man.

In my financial planning practice, I used to hate the idea of selling life insurance. I was embarrassed. I bought into the stereotype of the pushy life insurance salesperson. I didn't understand the importance of the product. I dealt with those internal battles for several years until a recently widowed client, Judy, was sitting in my office.

After spending a few minutes talking about her late husband, Jerry, she said, "Michael, what am I gonna do? These people depend on me. How am I going to keep my business going and stay in my house?"

I said, "I know this won't replace Jerry, and in your grief, you've probably forgotten how much insurance he had." I reached across the desk and handed her a life insurance proceeds check in the amount of $600,000.

She took the check and stared at it for two or three minutes. A wave of every conceivable emotion swept across her face in that period of time. Finally, she said, "I'm going to be able to keep my business. My people can keep their jobs. I can keep my house."

In that moment, I knew the importance of selling life insurance. I never again felt the embarrassment or felt put-off by selling it. That scene represented a major internal change for me.

What makes a great climactic scene? It must include either a significant event or the lesson that was learned. Often, it includes both.

What is a significant event? It could be any number of incidents—a health crisis, a natural disaster, or an unexpected change in a relationship. Any of these can be a catalyst to change your character's point of view.

For your climax to be most effective, there is one other key. *You* should not be the source of the knowledge or lesson learned. Why?

Think about speakers you've heard who spent most of their time telling you how intelligent they are or how successful or how they had all the answers to your troubles. What type of feeling did you have after listening to those people?

My guess is that it wasn't good. As you've read in previous lessons, **when you build yourself up, you also build a wall between you and your audience**. Not taking credit for the wisdom you share is not always easy on the ego, but it is vital that you follow this advice. Otherwise, you lose your connection and believability with your audience.

Imagine if miserable old Scrooge had gone to bed one night, woke up the next morning, sat up in bed, stretched, and then said, "Ya know what? I've been a real schmuck! These people deserve to be treated better. I need to apologize and change my ways. It took me a long time, but I finally figured it out all on my own!"

Not really believable, is it? And it wouldn't make for much of a play. No one changes that much without some outside assistance. In "A Christmas Carol," the ghosts should and do get all the credit for Scrooge's change.

As you create your climax, who can serve as your "ghosts"? You've learned lessons from other people, books, and events. Give them the credit, and the audience will want to hear more.

When you develop the climax to your story, give the audience what they want. Share the lesson learned. Let them know how it has changed your life. Tell them how it can change theirs, too. And be sure that you are not the source of this newfound wisdom.

Incorporate these steps, and your journey to developing a meaningful and memorable story is nearly complete.

**ACTION STEP:** Create the climactic scene to your story. Be sure to answer the key audience questions discussed in this lesson. Also, give credit to whomever or whatever taught you the lesson.

**RECOMMENDED RESOURCE:** A book that, on the surface, has nothing to do with storytelling or speaking: *The Power of NICE,* by Linda Kaplan Thaler and Robin Koval. It's a great read because it discusses the power of treating others with respect and kindness. Although the focus of this book is more on interpersonal communication, the lessons apply to your role as speaker or storyteller.

When you treat your audience with respect, communicate with them as you would your friends, and carry the belief that telling your story to others is a privilege, people will pick up on your attitude and listen to what you have to say. To get your copy, visit: http://amzn.to/1oarZXL.

# Step 26 - **No Change, No Sale**

In the last chapter, we talked about the importance of a climax and the change that the character experiences. As Craig Valentine has said, "if there is *no change*, there is *no sale*." You won't sell your main message to the audience if there isn't a change in your characters. Let's explore this concept further.

In one of the key scenes in the movie "It's a Wonderful Life," banker George Bailey (portrayed by Jimmy Stewart), sees what life would have been like if he'd never been born. This leads him to the realization that his life is worth living and that he has had a positive impact on many lives.

Imagine if, after seeing this "alternate universe," George had still dashed out of his home toward the bridge and jumped into the icy waters to his death. Besides being a bummer of an ending to the movie, there would have been an overriding question: "What was the point? He killed himself anyway!" Great question.

There would have been no point. George would not have experienced any change in perspective. He would be the same person at the end of the story as he was at the beginning. Neither he nor the audience would have bought into the message that *it's a wonderful life.*

Unfortunately, this is a common problem for many presenters. They tell stories, describe characters, explain circumstances, but then fail to describe the changes that were experienced.

If your purpose in telling stories is to change the way an audience Thinks, Feels, or Acts, then doesn't it make sense to give them the ultimate benefit of the tools or processes that you're teaching? That benefit is couched in the changes in your characters.

For example, the birth of your first child probably changed your perspective on responsibility; experiencing a bankruptcy may have changed the manner in which you handle money; overcoming a lifelong fear may have helped you find faith or courage that had been long buried. These outcomes can provide the audience with hope that they, too, can experience the same results.

George Bailey experienced a major shift in attitude when he realized his life was worthwhile. Your stories and your lessons may not be as dramatic as his, but you have learned lessons that could change the lives of your audience.

Don't forget to allow your audience to see the transformation that your characters experienced. When you talk about these changes, your audience, like George Bailey, may just come to the conclusion, "What a wonderful message!" When they see the change, consider your message *sold!*

**ACTION STEP:** Review your story to be sure that you have shown the change that your character has experienced. It's good practice to remind the audience of where the character was, and how differently he now sees the world after experiencing the change. Tie that to your overriding message to ensure consistency in your story.

**RECOMMENDED RESOURCE:** The book, *Speak Like Churchill, Stand Like Lincoln*, by James C. Humes. Mr. Humes is a former Presidential speechwriter. He offers insight into two of the most eloquent and influential speakers in history. Through his 21 "Power" lessons, Humes shares tools and strategies used by these two great leaders to create messages that still resonate today. To get your copy, visit: http://amzn.to/1sKDhmL.

# Step 27 - The Heart of Your Story

A speaker, after diligently preparing and practicing a content-rich speech, presents to her audience. She confidently shares her information and stories, and then concludes to scattered, polite applause. What happened? She described her characters and the circumstances they were in, and she talked about the changes they went through. She even told the audience how they would benefit from the main message.

Unfortunately, in spite of the speaker's best efforts, hers was not an unusual result. No matter how much work and preparation has gone into the material, it's all for naught if the delivery is not up to par. That's why this next tool is critical to story development. Some of the best speakers in the world believe that it is the *heart* of storytelling. That tool is *dialogue.*

As I have said, most speakers give you a report like a journalist: "John did this" or "Sally said that." Like I demonstrated in Step 22, dialogue shares the story from the perspective of the characters involved. The two approaches have a very different impact on the audience.

Consider these descriptions of the same story, one in monologue and one in dialogue:

**Version 1:** *Janet was visiting with her client Mary, who was elderly and lived alone. She told Janet how much her new wood floors meant to her. Janet seemed surprised; after all, these were floor coverings, not major surgery. Mary explained that, at her age, little things like nice floors make all the difference in your life.*

**Version 2:** *Janet was visiting with her client Mary, who said, "Janet, I can't tell you how much my new floor means to me. You have changed my life."*

*"Mary, that's very kind of you. But really? It's only floor covering."*

Mary said, *"Oh, Honey, you don't understand. I'm 87 years old. I live alone, and I don't get out much anymore. I've lived in this house for 46 years. When you have to look at the same worn-out floors and rugs all the time, it's depressing. Now, when I walk into my family room, I feel good. It's beautiful and clean, and it just makes me happy. When you get to be my age, you'll understand."*

Of the two delivery styles, which one makes you feel more like you were in the scene? If you said number 1, go back and read it again. Obviously, option 2 is the correct answer. But why?

When you *retell* a story, as in version one, you're giving an outsider's view. The information is factual, and it may create a picture in the listeners' minds, but it doesn't emotionally pull them in. It's more of a left-brain approach.

When you use dialogue, as in version two, the story comes to life. You engage more of the audience's imagination, more of the right brain. Say the line from the point of view of the characters, and your audience feels as if they're in the scene. This feeling is enhanced when characters describe details.

For example, in just a few short sentences from Mary, you learn these facts about her:

- She's 87 years old.
- She lives alone.
- She's lived in the same house for 46 years.
- She doesn't get out much.
- Clean and beautiful floors are some of those "little things" that are very important to someone her age.

You learned all of that in 106 words of dialogue! This is much more effective and creates more audience involvement than reporting the facts, as in, "Mary is an elderly woman. She lives alone. She loves her new floor coverings."

Don't make the mistake that most speakers make—avoid being a reporter. Instead, give your story dialogue. You can easily stand out from most presenters if you employ this one tool. It will add life to your stories and turn them into an experience that your audiences will not soon forget.

**ACTION STEP:** As you create interaction between your characters, look for every opportunity to turn monologue into dialogue. The more details your characters can give through this dialogue, the more of an experience you will create. Also, ask if the dialogue you're creating sounds like the words people would actually use. This enforces the believability of each statement.

**RECOMMENDED RESOURCE:** The book, *The Writers Journey: Mythic Structure for Writers*, by Christopher Vogler. Mr. Vogler is a well-known Hollywood screenwriter who has thoroughly studied the history of mythology and stories. He offers insight into why movies like "Star Wars" and "Titanic" share common threads with stories told throughout human history. This is a great read to help you understand common links of stories that survive through the ages. To get your copy, visit: http://amzn.to/1mvIaDI.

# Step 28 - Get in Their Heads

In the last chapter, you learned about the importance of dialogue. Conversations between characters give insight into your story, their background, and the circumstances of that story.

Conversations between characters are not your only source of dialogue, though. Your audience can gain insight by hearing the inner thoughts of characters. For example, in my story about getting engaged in a cornfield, I describe the scene where my girlfriend Linda and I are driving along, when she suddenly stops the car, puts it in park, opens her door, jumps out, and runs into a cornfield.

At that point, I could say, "I felt so exasperated that I didn't know what to do. That's when I heard a voice tell me to propose right then and there."

Instead, I share my inner thoughts. "What in the *world* is she doing? What is going on? This day has been a disaster!"

That's when I heard a voice say, "Do it *now*!"

I thought, "What?"

"Look at her smile. She's so happy. Do it *now*!"

Can you see the difference? In the first version, I'm in reporter mode. In the second, you have insight into my thoughts and feelings. Doesn't this make you feel like you're in the moment, and don't you feel my frustration?

Give the audience insight into your thoughts, and you make them more emotionally involved in the story.

There is another tool that creates the same kind of connection. Put the *audience's thoughts* into your story. When you verbalize the ideas that run through their minds, you elevate yourself because they feel you're talking directly to them and that you know exactly how they're feeling.

The following example demonstrates this effect:

In our 3D Storytelling workshop, I discuss the importance of pausing when delivering your message. I could say: "It's important to pause for several seconds to allow people time to think about your points or laugh at your humor. Most people struggle with this. They're uncomfortable with silence. You may be, too. You may feel a lack of confidence or uncertainty about staying quiet that long."

Instead, what I say is: "It's important to pause for several seconds to allow people time to think about your points or laugh at your humor. I know what you may be thinking. 'Are you nuts, Mike? Several seconds! I can't do that. If I stand there saying nothing, I'm gonna look ridiculous. That may work for you, but I could never do that!' Don't worry. That's a natural feeling. I promise you that's what you'll be thinking the first time you try pausing that long. When it happens, try to remember this piece of advice: Pause until it hurts; then, add one second. This is not a skill you master overnight; it takes practice."

What happens when you say something like this? Audience members think, "S/he knows what I'm thinking. S/he knows how I feel." When audiences think this way, you've made a deeper connection, and they're open to everything you have to say after that.

Dialogue is a terrific tool to put audience members in your scenes, but don't limit yourself to dialogue between characters. Give insight into your own thoughts, and give your audience a hint that you know what they're thinking and feeling. You'll bring them even deeper into your world.

**ACTION STEP:** As you build your story, create inner dialogue for your characters to give insight into their thoughts and feelings. Also, look for opportunities to let the audience know you understand *their* thoughts and feelings.

**RECOMMENDED RESOURCE:** The book, *Writing Dialogue*, by Tom Chiarella. This resource offers ideas on writing dialogue in fiction and compares this to writing in normal conversational style. Even if you're only writing for your speeches, this book offers insight into writing better, more believable dialogue. To get your copy, visit: http://amzn.to/1EKUuav.

# Step 29 - Is Your Language Turning Off Your Audience?

"For so many years, I've yearned to speak professionally, to be sought out, to share my years of transgressions, my foibles, and my ultimate victories. In the aftermath of the termination of my marriage, I have nothing but this empty abode. Why not take the risk; why not pursue my great dream? I haven't a thing to lose."

Question. Does this sound like something you'd hear in a normal conversation? Or does it sound more like something you'd read in a novel? Read it again...

"For so many years, I've yearned to speak professionally, to be sought out, to share my years of transgressions, my foibles, and my ultimate victories. In the aftermath of the termination of my marriage, I have nothing but this empty abode. Why not take the risk; why not pursue my great dream? I haven't a thing to lose."

There's a pretty good chance you would never talk like this, and neither would your friends. One of my first speech coaches called this using 25-dollar words when 25-cent words will do.

Far too often, speakers write stories with dialogue that sounds as if it belongs in a Dickens or Harlequin romance novel. In the example you just read, the language may have been exaggerated just a tad, but hopefully, the point is made. I've heard speakers try to impress an audience with over-the-top language. I would ask them the same question: Who talks like this?

In a novel, you might get away with this, but it won't work for a speech or in a story you tell. Rob Friedman, executive director of communications for Eli Lilly and Company, says you should "Writing should not be for the page, but for the ear." [xvii]

Writing for the ear means that you write conversationally, the way you would speak in dialogue with a friend, or maybe even in your head.

What if the paragraph above was translated into everyday English?

"I stood alone in my empty apartment and thought, 'You've lost everything! Well, yeah, the divorce wiped me out... You ready to be a professional speaker now? I guess I've got nothin' to lose.'"

Don't those words sound more conversational? This is a conversation that took place in my head on the day I moved into my apartment after my marriage ended.

Is that conversation believable? It should be because that's how it unfolded in my head.

If the dialogue in your speech is conversational, it's more believable. Fighting the urge to sound high-brow or to come across as highly intelligent can be challenging, but if you invest the time, you'll gain more credibility.

This challenge is especially true in the corporate world. There are many sites on the Internet devoted to sharing examples of corporate-speak. Check them out. Although they are humorous, ask yourself if you've ever been caught in the trap of using this type of language.

It's easy to fall into the world of corporate-speak when you're surrounded by it all day. When you prepare your presentations, remember that your audience simply wants you to talk like someone sitting across from them at the dinner table.

For example, at work, you may hear phrases like, "The amount of good will carried on the balance sheet, when compared to total assets, is high." When you share this with your family or friends, translate it into English. Just say, "Our company overpaid for the last few companies they bought."

As you write your dialogue, ask one question: "Is this how people really talk, or am I trying to sound impressive?" Test your dialogue with friends and family, with business colleagues, or at your next NSA or Toastmasters meeting. The feedback you receive will tell you whether you're on track or need to make adjustments.

If you write dialogue that is believable and sounds conversational, you will stand out from the crowd.

**ACTION STEP:** Review the dialogue you've written for your stories. Determine whether the words and sentences sound like phrases that would take place in normal conversation or if they belong in a novel. Ask others to evaluate you and point out what needs to be changed.

**RECOMMENDED RESOURCE:** An article entitled "Activating Your Active Voice" written by Randy Harvey. Randy is a true student of the art of speaking. He is especially gifted in "wordsmithing" - finding those words and sentences that have an impact on an audience but still sound conversational. This article offers insight into how you can write in a way that is easy on your audience and makes it effortless for them to follow your story. To read this article, visit: http://bit.ly/1tfYJ7U.

# Step 30 - Take Them on a Roller Coaster

Ever ridden a roller coaster? What makes it exciting? For many, it's the contrasting ups and downs - the anticipation of rocketing down the first big hill, the temporary relief at the bottom, and the rebuilding of anticipation for the next hill. It's what makes the ride so thrilling.

A great speech can provide the same effect.

I recently learned this from Randy Harvey. He showed me how he used a "roller coaster" effect to create his world championship speech.

One of the problems that Randy's strategy remedies is the tendency to jump too quickly into an emotional story before "earning" the audience's trust.

Many audience members are skeptical when you begin speaking. They may be concerned that you will try to sell them something or attempt to manipulate their emotions. It's important to develop rapport to encourage them to open up emotionally and allow you to share deeply personal stories.

At this point, visit the link http://bit.ly/129ssVV to watch Randy's speech.

How did Randy demonstrate the roller coaster effect in his speech?

He opened with an amusing tale of standing on top of a car to escape a pack of dogs. He used humor to open the audience up to his first "mini" point, which he shared through his father's words.

He gave you just enough to be willing to hear more, then set you up for his second story - an amusing anecdote about he and his friends talking about girls. Once again, his father shared an important life lesson that was a little deeper than the first.

Because of his expert combination of humor and key points, he made you ready to hear his walkaway message, which he shared through his third story.

It is a touching story that underscores his main point about love. Notice in particular how Randy expertly introduced the subject of death (twice) without ever using the word "death" or sounding maudlin or overly dramatic.

This story is a rare example of a serious and potentially negative subject told in a manner that leaves you on an "up" note. The end result is a speech that is entertaining, touches hearts, and leaves the audience with an impactful message. Ten years later, people still talk about his speech. And Randy accomplished this in just seven minutes (not counting the hundreds of hours of preparation and practice).

When you create your next speech, think about the roller coaster. How can you arrange your stories in a manner that takes your audience to a deeper level with each succeeding story? Take your audience on the roller coaster, and give them a ride they'll never forget.

**ACTION STEP**: Watch Randy Harvey's World Championship speech entitled "Fat Dad." Pay attention to the emotional impact he makes on the audience as he shares each story. Use his speech as a template to write your next speech with the roller coaster effect.

**RECOMMENDED RESOURCE:** Randy Harvey's book, *Public Speaking 101: Messages That Matter.* Randy is one of the best students of public speaking I've ever met. In addition to the roller coaster approach he personally taught me, I've picked up many other ideas from this book. Use his "SCREAM" strategy in particular, and you'll set your speech apart from others. To get your copy, visit: http://amzn.to/UGMtzr.

# Step 31 - Arrive Late, Leave Early

When setting up and sharing their stories, most speakers share far too many details. The result is that audiences can get bored and check out mentally and emotionally.

On the opposite end of the spectrum, many speakers share too much information long after the point has been made. The result is often the same—bored audience.

The solution to this problem is called "Arrive Late, Leave Early." This term was coined by screenwriter William Goldman in his book *Adventures in the Screen Trade*[xviii]. This concept introduces the audience to a story very close to it's climax scene. Remember, this is the part that sets up the key to your tale - the change.

For example, in my story, "Cornfield Wisdom," you hear about a frustrating day when my best laid plans for the "perfect engagement" fell apart. It was almost out of desperation that I asked my girlfriend, Linda, to marry me while we were standing in a cornfield.

The challenge in writing the story was to avoid all of the details leading up to that moment—the rental property we had to deal with that morning because of a burst water pipe; the hours I spent creating the perfect songs for the occasion, only to forget my iPod that day; and my last-minute discovery that Linda's favorite flowers weren't available in Cincinnati, Ohio in late August. That destroyed my plans for a room full of tulips for the big moment. Unfortunately, those weren't the only problems that day. But you get the idea.

Each of those was a reason why my plans fell apart and why my frustration kept building. But those details aren't important to the audience. What they need to know is that I wanted to have the perfect proposal, my day fell apart, and I ended up asking her in a cornfield. They also need to know that I learned an important lesson because my original plan fell apart. Oh, I guess they also want to know if she said "yes."

This is how I now open that story: "I was sitting in the passenger seat of my girlfriend, Linda's car. She was standing 30-feet away in a cornfield.

'What are we doing here? This is a disaster—the flood at the house, I forgot the iPod, couldn't get the flowers. Nothing has gone right today!'

That's when a little voice said, 'Do it now.'

I said, 'In a cornfield?'

'Yes, look at that smile on her face. She's so happy. Do it now.'

I thought, "Well... why not? I've got nothing to lose.'

I slowly got out of the car, and walked over to ask the *big* question."

In 30 seconds, I set the stage without details you don't care about. The scene is flavored with just enough information to arouse your curiosity. It sets the stage for the big moment that could change my life.

It takes practice and feedback to whittle a scene down to its essence. That's why it's critical that you share your story with others and get feedback.

*What slowed the story down?*
*What details are unimportant to you?*
*Which ones kept your attention?*

The answers to those questions will help you get to the essence of your story.

At the other end, don't make the common mistake of giving details long after the point has been made. In the cornfield story, the climax occurs when, over dinner, I tell Linda, "I'm sorry, Honey. I had the whole day planned out, and *nothing* went right. I wanted it to be the perfect proposal."

She said, "Michael, you don't understand. I love spontaneity. I love cornfields. I love *you*. It *was* the perfect proposal."

At the end of my story, I say: "That was the moment I realized that I had been looking at this all wrong. I was seeing it through my eyes, what I wanted, and not Linda's eyes. That was a valuable lesson for me."

In less than 45 seconds, the point of the story is made. There's no need to add more. Unfortunately, many speakers keep telling you more about what they ate for dinner, how they went out afterward for celebratory cocktails and dancing. *None* of those details adds to the message.

After the climactic scene and the change in the character(s) is revealed, remind the audience of the walk-away message, offer them a next step, and end the story.

*Arrive late, leave early.* This concept will help you create interest faster and leave the audience with a meaningful message. Just as important, they'll be thankful that you were clear and didn't take a long time to do it. That alone will make you memorable.

**ACTION STEP:** Share your story with others. Ask for feedback about extraneous details that bog down the opening and take away from the strength of your conclusion. Ask others to help you pare the story down to its essential elements.

Also, listen to other stories, and determine which parts you think are unnecessary. This practice will help you spot details that move a story forward or bog it down.

**RECOMMENDED RESOURCE:** The book, *Save the Cat,* by Blake Snyder. Ostensibly, this book was written for screenwriters, but Mr. Snyder shares ideas on how to create a connection between characters and audience members. The title is born from the idea that if your character does something nice in the beginning of the story, such as rescuing a cat from a tree, it builds likability for that person. It's what Patricia Fripp calls a "rooting interest." To get your copy, visit: http://amzn.to/XQ6B2x.

# Step 32 - **Open With a BANG!**

When you start a presentation, what are the first words out of your mouth? "Thank you, ladies and gentlemen. It's a pleasure to be here. Isn't this great weather? What a great crowd." Or do you say some variation of those words? If you're opening your speeches or stories this way, I encourage you to heed these two words of advice:

STOP!
PLEASE!!

Why such an over-the-top reaction? Because I don't want you to fall into the trap that most speakers fall into—opening with boring platitudes. When you open your story this way, you sound like every other presenter.

To quote Patricia Fripp, "Audiences will forgive almost anything except being boring. Open with a BANG!" [xix] Starting your presentation with thank yous or a discussion of the weather is dull and deadly boring.

Research has shown that you have less than 30 seconds to make an impression on an audience. In fact, before you ever walk to the front of a room, you're being judged—your appearance, the expression on your face, how confident you appear, etc. Is this fair?? Nope. But it's a fact, and it's one you must be aware of if you want to make a *Stand OUT!* first impression.

What can you do to make an impact in the first few seconds? Ms. Fripp suggests "The first thirty seconds have the most impact. Don't waste these precious seconds with "Ladies and Gentlemen" or a weather report. Come out punching!" [xx] This means that you do or say something that is different and grabs the audience's attention.

Jumping into your story is typically the best way to start. However, the following options can also be effective:

1) Recite a quote.
2) Ask a question.
3) Make a startling statement.
4) Introduce a statistic.

Each of these can be very effective tools to setting up your story.

In Step 21, you learned the importance of setting context. At first glance, these ideas of how to open your story might seem to contradict the suggestion of setting context.

The key is that these openings must be relevant to both your story and your main point. Properly structured, they will also set the context.

For example, in my *Cornfield Wisdom* speech, I have opened it with the question, "Have you ever had a frustrating day teach an important life lesson?" I've also used the statement "This is a disaster—the flood at the house, I forgot the iPod, couldn't get the flowers. Nothing has gone right today! As frustrating as that day was, it taught me a valuable lesson about capitalizing on unexpected opportunities."

Each of these grabs the audience's attention, and provides context for the story and message that follows.

Far too often, speakers recite quotes or make statements that are irrelevant to the overall presentation. These may get a quick nod of agreement or a laugh, but they'll be quickly forgotten.

My favorite method for opening a presentation is the most rarely used, yet extremely effective. It is: Silence. Why would you use silence to start a presentation? Don't you want to go up there full of energy and "come out punching"?

Yes, you do. However, think about an audience when you stand at the front of a room. Most likely, they're shifting in their seats, rustling papers, or thinking about what the last speaker had to say or dozens of other thoughts running through their heads. Chances are, they're not focused on you when you first get to the front of a room.

When you stand before them, quietly, confidently, and with a smile on your face, make eye contact with as many as possible. Then, you'll get their attention. When you can do this for five to seven seconds and feel your audience become drawn to you, it's a powerful feeling.

*I warn you*, however. The first time you try to do this, you won't last two seconds! You'll feel uncomfortable, scared, and maybe even stupid. Ask me how I know this. I felt all of those emotions the first few times I tried it. But when I stood for one or two seconds the first time and added a second each successive time, within just a few speeches, I got very comfortable opening with a pause.

Whether you pause, use a story, a quote, or a question, make sure it relates to your main point. Nothing confuses a group more than mixed messages. Your opening can make or break your presentation. When you open with the same platitudes that every other speaker uses, the audience is already beginning to tune you out because their first impression will be that you're just like everyone else.

Experiment with the different ideas you've learned here. You can grab the audience's attention and set them up for your message when you open with a BANG!

**ACTION STEP:** Review the opening of your presentation. Get audience feedback. Is it memorable? Does it grab their attention? Try different methods—a quote, a startling statement, or a question to set up your story. And don't be afraid to use the most powerful tool of all—silence. Test your openings, and let the audience tell you which one works best.

**RECOMMENDED RESOURCE:** A YouTube video entitled "Circular Technique" by Patricia Fripp. In this video, she focuses on a specific process to open your speech—the circular technique. This is a method that ties your opening and conclusion together. Watch this video, and enjoy a master who many consider to be the best speaking coach in the world. Visit http://bit.ly/ZXZKWr to watch the video.

# Step 33 - Leave 'em Wanting More

*Get off stage ... leave 'em on a high note.*

That's an old adage in the comedy world for when you get a huge laugh from the audience. A similar sentiment in the speaking world is that you should never give an audience everything you've got. Give them good ideas, share some great stories, a next step, and then get off stage. *Leave 'em wanting more.*

This is an area where most presenters fall flat. I've seen great speakers ruin an otherwise terrific presentation by ending their talk with a very forgettable conclusion.

Why is it important to conclude on a strong note? In the words of Patricia Fripp, "Last words linger." [xxi] The audience is more likely to remember your main point if your final words tie to that message ... and they're memorable.

Before you hear the best ways to conclude, it's important that you avoid two of the biggest conclusion mistakes made by speakers. The first is that they introduce new material near the end.

You've probably heard a presentation where the speaker seemed to be ready to wrap up, gave what you thought were concluding remarks, and then introduced something new that left you confused. "Why are these new ideas being introduced so close to the end?" you probably thought.

Imagine if, after the conclusion of one of the greatest speeches in American history, Dr. Martin Luther King, had said, "Free at last, free at last, thank God almighty we are free at last .... and another thing, we've got to do something about our educational system." People would have been incredibly confused, and the power of that legendary final sentence would have been severely diminished.

The second and even bigger error that presenters make is that they end with Questions and Answers (Q&A). Why is this a mistake? Imagine that a speaker has come out punching with her opening. She's used memorable stories to support a very powerful point. Then, she has given a strong final statement and opens the floor to questions.

When this happens, you lose control of your speech. You don't know what type of questions will be asked. You can't control the tone of those questions. They may be relevant or irrelevant to your point. The questioner could be combative, or the question could simply leave the audience confused. When you give up control in this manner, you have no idea if the audience will remember your final words or if they'll walk away puzzled.

How should you use Q&A, and what is a better way to conclude? If you're going to have a Q&A session, do it five to ten minutes before you end. Set it up with a time limit and not by the number of questions. If you say "I've got time for two questions," and those two questions are each five minutes long, you've got a problem.

Instead, say, "We've got five minutes for questions, and then we'll close. I'll be here afterward if you want to talk further." This lets them know that you're about to conclude. It leaves you in control and allows you to set up your concluding statement.

Once you've answered questions, how do you finish? As Patricia Fripp discussed in the educational resource video recommended in the last chapter, the circle back technique is effective. "Circling back" means you return to your opening comments. If you asked a question in the opening, you could answer that question or revisit it from a different perspective. If it was a quote or comment, restate it from the perspective of the material that you presented in your speech.

Using questions, quotes, or comments to conclude are effective methods to leave the audience thinking about your message. It's critical that these are related to your main point. Otherwise, your message is lost.

Concluding your presentation is a skill. If you want the audience to remember your story and your main point, end on a high note. Use a statement or question that ties to your main theme, and you will leave 'em wanting more.

**ACTION STEP:** Develop a conclusion to your story that reinforces your message. Use a statement, question, or quote that supports this point. Remember, do *not* conclude with Q&A or introduce new information at the end of your presentation. The Circle Back process is an excellent tool to tie your opening and supporting material to your ending.

**RECOMMENDED RESOURCE:** A brief YouTube video entitled "How to Write a Speech Conclusion" from Darren LaCroix. Darren reinforces ideas learned in this lesson and offers additional suggestions on how to wrap up with power and on a high note. Visit http://bit.ly/1tIfvOd to watch the video.

# Part 3

# How to Deliver Your *Stand OUT!* Stories

# Step 34 - **Break the Rules, Part 2**

So far, you've learned tools and processes to develop your stories. The coming chapters will focus more on the third dimension of the 3D Storytelling process - *Deliver your stories.* Do this in a dynamic style and people will remember your message long after you speak.

In Step 18, you read about breaking the rules. More than in any other area of presenting and storytelling, there are delivery "rules" that have been passed down for years. Unfortunately, because most people use these techniques, they're no longer unique. The individuals who use them now all look and sound alike.

Here are some examples of the "rules" most speakers follow:

- If you get nervous, imagine people in their underwear.
- If you're uncomfortable looking at the audience, look just over the tops of their heads at a spot on the back wall.
- Memorize your speech because using notes makes you look unprofessional.
- Try to look every audience member in the eye at some point during your speech.

- Come out with 100% energy to pump them up.
- Start with a joke.

Why should you avoid these? They don't help you make the best possible connection. Imagining people in their underwear or looking over the tops of their heads will disengage you from the audience. Being present by seeing them as they are, talking conversationally, and looking people in the eyes will help them feel a connection to you. Trying to make eye contact with absolutely everyone, however, shifts your focus from your message, is unrealistic and will distract you from connecting with your audience as a whole.

When you try to memorize every word of your speech, your focus is on the wrong place. You're worried about you and not capable of reading your audience members' reactions and body language. Knowing your main point, supporting stories and concepts, opening, and conclusion will help you create memorable talks and allow you to focus on your audience.

Opening with full-on energy can be a risk for two reasons. If you start at 100% energy, you've got nowhere to go but down. Although the opening is where you make your initial connection, it isn't where you make your key points or where the audience will buy into your message. You increase your odds of making a long-lasting impact by raising and lowering your energy as the story dictates.

Also, it's important to match the energy level of your audience. If you're speaking to an early-morning audience that needs coffee just to be awake, they're not going to be eager to listen to an overenthusiastic presenter, at least not until they're more alert and you've connected with them.

As we move into the delivery phase of presenting your story, keep these ideas in mind. A key aspect of delivering effectively is to understand your own style and to present your story in a manner that feels natural to you. In the coming chapters, you'll learn how to do that. As you uncover your style along the way, always remember that it's OK to break a few rules.

**ACTION STEP / RECOMMENDED RESOURCE:** Your action step and recommended resource this week are one and the same. Visit YouTube.com and watch other speakers. Look for the common delivery techniques or strategies that most speakers use. These are techniques you want to avoid. Find speakers with a unique delivery style. Don't try to emulate them, but observe how they're different and how they stand out. Noticing unique delivery features of other presenters can help you start to uncover your own style.

Some speakers I suggest are: Les Brown, Tony Robbins, Patricia Fripp, Darren LaCroix, Craig Valentine, Ed Tate, and Jeanne Robertson.

# Step 35 - **Move with a Purpose**

A speaker with a strong presence prowls the room like a caged tiger. He moves from left to right, then right to left, crisscrossing the room. For added entertainment, he holds a writing pen in his right hand and clicks the pen each time he stops and pivots to move in a different direction. This continues until you are lulled into a semi-coma.

What is the result of this constant movement? You don't retain anything the speaker says, you grow tired, and you might even need to hit the coffee machine to make it through the rest of your day.

Unfortunately, this is probably the most common delivery mistake made by speakers. Some of the best presenters have this habit. Even worse, many are aware of the problem but still do it! Why?

The most common reason is nerves. Speakers who don't learn how to control their nerves release that energy in front of their audiences. The result is frustration for audiences because they're distracted by this unnecessary, constant motion.

The other reason for this pacing is that many presenters don't understand how to use the speaking area as part of their story. Properly used, it can serve as a prop to make your story more of an experience.

What is the solution to this pacing habit? A common mantra in the speaking world is to **Move with a Purpose**. To do this, there are three steps:

1. **Know your material.** When you've internalized (not memorized) your message, you'll be in the moment and can be more aware of where you are on the platform. If you have to think about what you're going to say, you'll probably move all over the speaking area and not be cognizant of unnecessary movement. You should always work on practicing and rehearsing the words you'll say before you focus on your delivery.

2. **Break your story into sections** that can be delivered from different parts of the speaking area. For example, when presenting my speech entitled "Trust the Car," my first story is told stage right to the audience's left; the second story is told stage center; and the third story is told stage left to the audience's right. This not only helps the audience compartmentalize each story, but allows me to point back to each place on the stage when referring to previous stories. The audience knows immediately what I'm referring to.

3. **Know where to deliver key points**. Most people simply continue to move around the stage while they deliver their points. To emphasize the importance of any key part of your story, however, it's best to move to the center part of the stage, plant your feet, lean forward, and state your point. This part of the stage is often referred to as the "power point." Please don't confuse that term with PowerPoint presentation software, though.

With enough repetition to internalize your message and your stories, you'll feel more comfortable using specific areas of the stage to match different parts of your story.

Early in my speaking career, I was always focused on giving perfect presentations. I pre-planned everywhere I would stand. Unfortunately, everything I did looked staged, and as a result, I didn't connect with my audiences. I wasn't comfortable with my own style.

It was only after watching other presenters, giving dozens of evaluations, and studying my own speeches, on both audio and video, that I began to understand and feel comfortable with who I am as a presenter. My style tends to be more energetic. I inject humor into many of my presentations, and I don't deliver speeches or stories that are overly emotional.

That's my style. I've grown very comfortable with it over 20 years. With time, practice, and repetition, you'll become familiar and comfortable in your own skin, so to speak.

**Extra Tip!** Before closing out this lesson, I offer you one final tip that can be a lifesaver if you ever have one of those moments when you forget what you were going to say. It's happened to the best of us! Before going on stage, strategically place a water bottle somewhere at the front of the room, perhaps on a lectern, table, or chair. If, at some point in your speech, you go blank, calmly walk over to the water bottle. Next to the bottle, you will have placed an outline of your speech. Pick up that water bottle, take a s-l-o-w and thoughtful drink, then glance down at your notes as you return the bottle to its perch.

That will be enough information to get you back on track. Go back to where you were standing when you went blank, and pick up your story where you left off.

Understand what's going on in the minds of the audience when you do this, however. Whatever your last sentence, they're thinking, "Wow, that's really important because the speaker paused long enough to go get a drink and really let us think about it."

**ACTION STEP:** Begin practicing the delivery of your presentation. Plot out which part of the stage belongs with each part of your story. It's critical to test this. Get into a Toastmasters club, and ask for feedback strictly on the delivery. Is the audience confused by where you're telling each part of the story, or is the location of your delivery consistent and congruent with the story?

**RECOMMENDED RESOURCE:** A YouTube video clip of 2012 World Champion of Public Speaking Ryan Avery. As you watch this video, notice how Ryan uses the stage to tell different parts of his story. Also, notice how he uses the center of the stage to open and conclude his speech. This is a fine example of a speaker who tells his story from different parts of the stage and keeps each part separate in the audience's mind. To watch the video, visit: http://bit.ly/1oY0Ltg.

# Step 36 - **Walk the Timeline**

In the last chapter, you learned the importance of moving with a purpose and speaking from strategically selected parts of the stage. Another staging process to use is the "timeline method." This allows your audience to experience the chronology of your story.

To be most effective, tell the beginning part of the story at the right of the stage (the audiences' left). As you progress through, physically move slightly toward stage left at each new point in the presentation. When you get to the last part of the story you should be standing stage left.

This process allows you to anchor each story or point to a specific part of the stage. This allows you to point to another part of the stage at any time during your talk to reference an earlier part of the story. You've clearly anchored that part of the stage to that aspect of the story, and your audience will know exactly what you mean.

For example, the stories in my speech *Cornfield Wisdom* are told chronologically. When I conclude that talk, I encourage the audience to be open to unexpected opportunities and be ready to take advantage of them. While doing so, I reference each story by pointing to the area of the stage where I delivered each one. The audience immediately recalls the story without my having to retell it or walk to that part of the speaking area.

Some speakers have used this timeline concept very effectively. Very few, though, use the entire stage to create a "3-dimensional (3D) effect ." This entails moving from front to back or back to front. Done effectively, a 3D approach can take your story to a whole new level.

Darren LaCroix is a master at this. In this week's action step, you'll find a link to Darren's world championship speech. He opens that talk with a back to-front movement that underscores his point and makes an immediate connection with the audience.

He asks, "Can you remember a moment when a brilliant idea flashed into your head? It was perfect for you. But then, all of a sudden, from the depths of your brain, another thought started forcing its way forward through the enthusiasm until it finally shouted...." [xxii]

When you watch Darren present his speech, notice how his movement on stage matches his words. When he talks about another thought forcing its way forward, he moves from the back of the stage toward the front.

This is the 3D effect, which creates a "you are there" feeling for the audience. Later in the speech, Darren also employs the timeline effect.

This speech is one of the best examples I have seen on using stage placement to share your stories and keep the audience engaged and entertained. I recommend you watch this several times to see a master use the platform to turn his story into an experience.

**ACTION STEP:** Review your story to determine how you can use the timeline and 3D processes to tell different aspects of your stories from various parts of the speaking area. Practice telling your stories or points from each of these areas.

**RECOMMENDED RESOURCE:** Watch Darren LaCroix's world championship speech entitled "Ouch!" Although there are many lessons you can pick up from this presentation, pay close attention to Darren's use of the timeline and 3D processes. You'll learn a tremendous amount from this man in just seven minutes. To watch this video, visit: http://bit.ly/1nOsAn2.

# Step 37 - The Heart of Your Story, Part 2

In Step 27, you read about the importance of dialogue when writing your story. In this chapter, you'll pick up tools on how to deliver that dialogue so that you create a memorable scene that keeps audiences on the edge of their seats.

Consider the following anecdote. As you read, imagine how the typical speaker conveys this type of story:

"Joe was livid with Jim and told him so. He was upset because Jim hadn't consulted him about the contract with the new client. Because of a detail Jim overlooked, the client had an escape clause, and she had exercised it. And that cost the company $143,400. Joe reminded Jim that was why they had processes in place. When Jim asked if they could sue because of services provided, Joe told him that the attorney's fees would eat up most of what they would recover. It was a lost cause."

Besides the fact that this is a narration with no dialogue, most speakers tell this type of story in a matter-of-fact style that doesn't put the audience into the hearts of the characters. You get the facts about what's happening, but do you feel as if you're in the story?

But when most speakers rewrite the scene using dialogue, they still fail to maximize the impact of it because they don't emphasize key words that convey the feelings of each person in the scene.

Take a look at the rewrites of the scene above. In Version 1, there is dialogue but no emphasis on any key words. Version 2 highlights the thoughts that emphasize the characters' deepest emotions:

**Version 1**

Joe stormed into Jim's office and said, "Why did you complete this contract with Jennifer Holding!?"

"We need it in by end of the month, Joe."

"But you didn't review it with me like I told you to!"

Jim said, "I know, but I reviewed everything with a fine-toothed comb ... twice. Everything's fine. She's on board."

"Of course, she's on board! She doesn't have to pay us!"

"What are you talking about, Joe?"

Joe said, "I just hung up with her. She informed me that she's exercising the escape clause on page 4. We're on the hook for $143,400, and she doesn't have to pay us."

Jim's face was white as a sheet as he said, "She ... she can't ... do that."

"Really? It's in writing. She can do it ... and she is! I can't believe you! This is why we have processes in place, Jim, so this kind of thing never happens!"

"Can't we sue her? She's broken the spirit of the agreement."

"Yeah, we can sue, and the attorneys keep most of the judgment—if we win, which is unlikely. You've cost us a lot of money on this deal, Jim. It's going to take months to get over this."

"Joe, I'm sorry."

How does this version with dialogue compare to the version which is strictly narration? You're much closer to the emotions of the scene, aren't you? The biggest problem with the second version is that most speakers deliver it without emphasis on the key words that drive home the emotions.

**Version 2**

Joe stormed into Jim's office and said, "Why did you complete this contract with Jennifer Holding!?"

"We **need it** in by end of the month, Joe."

"But you didn't review it with me **like I told you to!**"

Jim said, "I know, but I reviewed **everything** with a fine-toothed comb ... **twice**. Everything's **fine**. She's on board."

"**Of course,** she's on board! She **doesn't have to pay us!**"

"What are you talking about, Joe?"

Joe said, "I just hung up with her. She informed me that she's exercising the escape clause on page 4. **We're on the hook for $143,400,** and she **doesn't have to pay us.**"

Jim's face was white as a sheet. He said, "She ... she **can't** ... do that."

"Really? It's in **writing**. She **can** do it ... and she **is!** I can't believe you! **This** is why we have processes in place, Jim, so this kind of thing **never** happens!"

"Can't we sue her? She's broken the spirit of the agreement."

"Yeah, we can sue ... and the attorneys keep **most** of the judgment—**if** we win, which is unlikely. You've cost us **a lot of money** on this deal, Jim. It's going to take **months** to get over this."

"Joe, I'm sorry."

How are you feeling about that version? A little uncomfortable? It's different than dialogue you'll hear in most stories, but it works in a speech that's focused on the importance of attention to details, the benefit of processes, or the need for collaboration.

There are six keys to take from this example that will most effectively make it work:

**1) Volume.** When recreating a scene, most speakers will say something like this: "I was really mad when I was told the event was cancelled" or "When Steve gave me the ring, I was ecstatic." They say these words in a monotone voice, with little or no emphasis on the key emotional words.

Be aware of the rise and fall of each character's emotions, and convey that. Let *your* voice be *their* voice.

**2) Tonality.** Much like volume, most speakers don't use tonality when using dialogue. In the previous examples, to convey the character's feelings, the speaker should either sound mad because the event was cancelled or sound ecstatic about getting the ring.

In the scene between Joe and Jim, the audience should *feel* Joe's anger and Jim's surprise, defensiveness, and disbelief, as well as the sincerity of Jim's apology at the end.

**3) Speed**. Use pace to convey emotion. People who are mad, excited, or nervous tend to speak *faster*. When they're sad, thoughtful, or relaxed, they talk in a *slower* pace. As you recreate dialogue, be aware of the pace that the emotion dictates.

**4) Speak conversationally**. Far too many speakers tell their story in the mode of speaker-man or speaker-woman. This hurts credibility because it doesn't feel genuine. As you become familiar with your story and comfortable conveying the emotions of the characters, aim to tell the story in a conversational style.

**5) Use character names in lines of dialogue.** So that the audience knows who is speaking, use the names of characters in sentences. If you're sharing an exchange between characters, you could confuse the audience if they're not sure who's speaking.

If you use the first four keys you've just learned, you'll eliminate the majority of the confusion. However, when you use the name of the recipient of the sentence in the conversation, you take the audience experience to a deeper level.

For example, in the exchange above, you heard these sentences:

"We need it by the end of the month, Joe."

"This is why we have processes in place, Jim."

"Can't we sue her, Joe?"

By dropping names into the conversation, you clearly distinguish who is speaking.

Of course, you don't want to do this in every sentence. That wouldn't sound like a realistic conversation. Do this just enough to make clear who the speaker is.

**6) Avoid sounding like a stage play.** This can happen when you avoid narration altogether. So, for every third or fourth line of dialogue, it's acceptable to use a set-up like "He said," or "Then, Jim asked," etc. This breaks up the dialogue just enough to provide a balanced mix of dialogue and narration.

Conversation is the heart of your story. When you incorporate the keys presented in this lesson, you will develop scenes that make people eager to hear the conclusion of your story and more of your message.

**ACTION STEP:** Review the conversations in your stories, and incorporate as many of the six keys as possible which were presented in this lesson. Test the dialogue, and ask for feedback to determine if the conversation sounds and feels authentic. Also, ask if there's any confusion about who the speakers are.

**RECOMMENDED RESOURCE:** Chapter 4 of the book, *World Class Speaking*, by Craig Valentine and Mitch Meyerson. This chapter focuses on processes and tools that will complement the delivery concepts you've learned. To get your copy, visit: http://amzn.to/1vvvgtO.

# Step 38 - **Warm Up**

Imagine a tennis pro walking onto the courts at Wimbledon without warming up. She just starts playing her match. How about a soccer player who runs onto the field without having stretched and prepared his body? It wouldn't make much sense, would it? Their minds and bodies wouldn't be ready for the strenuous task ahead, and they wouldn't perform at their best. For mental focus and to play at peak physical level, these athletes must warm up.

The same can be said for speakers. If you don't get yourself into "playing shape," you won't give your best performance. What do the best speakers and storytellers do to get themselves ready?

**1) Hydration**. In order to work at their best, your vocal cords need to be hydrated. The time to begin this is the day before you speak. If you wait until right before you walk on stage, it's too late. The body needs time to absorb the water and lubricate your vocal cords.

Water is by far the best liquid to ingest. Some fluids to avoid are caffeine and alcohol, as they tend to dry out the vocal cords. Milk or milk products should be avoided, too, because they produce mucous that makes clear diction more difficult. Also, avoid cold beverages because they can tighten and restrict the vocal cords.

**2) Breathing.** Breath or lack of it can make or break your presentation. If your air passages are clear and your lungs completely filled with air, you enunciate better, you'll have greater vocal range, and you will have more energy to get through your talk.

The late speaking coach, Ron Arden, pointed out that our lungs are somewhat pear-shaped, so it's important to open up the top half as much as possible. He suggested the 4:8:4:4 exercise. Breathe in for 4 seconds; hold it for 8 seconds; exhale for 4 seconds; wait 4 seconds; then, repeat the process five times. You'll find that your lungs are more open, and you're better prepared to speak.

**3) Music and exercise.** Music can energize you, and exercise helps burn off excess nervous energy. What music works best? Any type that pumps you up, but avoid funeral dirges or country songs about cheating spouses, lost jobs, or dogs running away. There's nothing wrong with those types of songs, but they set a less than stellar emotional tone.

There are many types of exercise that work well, including jumping jacks, push-ups, and walking up and down stairs. I've even danced before walking on stage. This is a great tool because it combines music and exercise. Try out different types of exercise to find one that works for you.

**4) Four questions**. I learned this from Darren LaCroix. [xxiii] To get centered on the audience, ask yourself these four questions five minutes before you step on stage:

1. What is my intent?
2. Will I have fun?
3. Am I present?
4. How would I give this presentation if I knew it was my last one ever?

In addition to getting your mind and body ready to speak, these tools will help you better manage your nerves. Feeling nervous is OK, however. It's only when you allow your nerves to control you that they become a problem.

After carefully researching the history of public speaking, and the overwhelming feelings of fear and stress that it can create, we've learned that no one has ever died from giving a speech.

Actually, that isn't true, technically speaking. The ninth President of the United States, William Henry Harrison, died from pleurisy and pneumonia after giving his inaugural address in a storm of snow and freezing rain. Like many men, he was stubborn and didn't wear adequate clothing that day. He caught a severe cold that developed quickly into his fatal illness. It should be noted that this really wasn't the fault of his speech; it was the foolish speaker who didn't listen to his mother and dress properly for his inauguration. But I digress.

Just like an athlete who needs to prepare for an important contest, you should prepare your mind and body before you speak. Use the ideas presented in this lesson, and you'll increase your odds of presenting at a peak level.

**Extra tip!** An additional exercise is one I learned from a local singer, Greg Anderson. Greg has been singing in rock bands in our city for over 30 years. He recently suggested that I hum my speech to warm up my vocal cords. It works! A word of warning, though. It sounds and feels ridiculous.

**ACTION STEP:** Test each of the four methods you learned in this lesson. Find the ones that work best for you. With repeated use, you'll develop your own preparation habits so that you can give your best effort every time.

**RECOMMENDED RESOURCE:** This time, I don't have a specific book or video. I simply suggest that you research Amazon.com to find materials about exercise, nutrition, and proper breathing. These subjects, when combined, can make you a better presenter *and* give you a better sense of well-being.

# Step 39 - Shut Up! Your Audience is Listening

Have you ever listened to a speaker who had great content, a dynamic style, and great enthusiasm, but you couldn't remember what s/he said or any details of the story?

How is that possible? With all of the speaker's positive attributes, how could s/he be so forgettable? Chances are, the speaker didn't understand the power of … silence. The talk was missing the effective use of pauses. I've already talked about the use of silence at the opening of your speech, but of all of the delivery tools at your disposal, pausing at key moments *throughout* your speech is one of the most misunderstood, underutilized, and under-appreciated.

When I ask audiences to tell me the most important delivery tool, I often hear "how you stand," "eye contact," or "gestures." Rarely, do they say "silence." Why is this so important? And why don't more speakers use it more effectively?

There are two main reasons. The first reason is that most speakers feel they must include as much information as possible in their presentations. So, they quickly move from one point to the next. This leaves no time for laughter or audience reflection. In Step 15, you read about this concept from a development standpoint - the idea of dropping a rock on your audience rather than skipping stones.

From a delivery standpoint, when you speak too quickly and don't allow your audience time to laugh or think about your points, you're, in essence, telling them to "be quiet." Would you do this in a one-on-one conversation? Probably not if you wanted to have any friends.

So, to maximize the impact of your message, it's important that you do one thing at critical points in your presentation: Shut up! Early in my speaking career, I was so concerned about what I was about to say next that I forgot this rule. The audience would start to laugh at my humorous lines, but I'd cut them off. After doing this a couple of times, they would stop laughing, or they would be interested in points I made but didn't connect with me. I just didn't allow them time to consider the implications of my points to their own lives. They became disinterested *bystanders* to my speech. Can you blame them? I was being rude.

The second reason for not using pauses is insecurity. Many speakers believe that if they aren't filling the quiet space, they'll lose audience attention. If you give people time to laugh or think about how your points will affect their lives, they open up to hear your deeper message. As Craig Valentine has said so eloquently, "The sale is in the silence."

Remember, a speech is a two-way conversation. The audiences' half of the conversation is their reflection. They may respond with a thoughtful "hmmm," a nod of the head, a tear, or a laugh. The effect is that you create a deeper connection, your speech becomes more of an experience, and they remember your takeaway message long after you speak. Not pausing is like repeatedly cutting them off in a conversation.

As you prepare your next presentation, build in time for laughter or reflection. This may necessitate cutting out some of your material, but is it more important to force-feed your audience with everything you know or create an environment that allows the audience to truly experience your message?

**ACTION STEP**: Review the written copy of your speech. Mark places where you can insert pauses. Then, practice those pauses. It won't be easy at first, but just like any other skill, the more you practice, the more comfortable you'll get. With this comfort and masterful use of silence, you'll see and feel the audience reaction.

**RECOMMENDED RESOURCE:** Rather than one specific resource, I recommend you visit two sites, You Tube and EdTate.com. Ed is the 2000 World Champion of Public Speaking, and a highly successful professional speaker. He is such a master of the pause that his fellow World Champions refer to lengthy pauses as 'The Ed Tate Scan.' Watch his videos, they're enlightening.

Additionally, I suggest you visit Ed's website because he offers a variety of resources for speaking, marketing, and running a speaking business.

# Step 40 - **The Look Before the Line**

In a previous lesson, you heard about the problem of being a reporter versus putting your audience into the scenes of your story. Another way to help your audience relive the experience of a story is to show the facial expressions of your characters before you deliver lines of dialogue.

Unfortunately, very few presenters do this. Most tell their stories in the following manner, with unchanging tonality or facial expressions:

"When I told my son, Jason, he would be going on the trip to Florida because of his straight A's, his face lit up. He got a huge grin. He was so thankful."

Or:

"Jenny was so mad. You could see it on her face. After a few seconds, she yelled at Jim and asked how he could spend so much on a motorcycle."

Is there anything wrong with this? No, but there are better ways to present these lines.

First, *set up the scene.* Describe the circumstances that led into the dialogue.

Second, instead of describing how a character feels, *demonstrate the emotion.* This is the concept I learned from Darren LaCroix. It's called "the Look Before the Line." This physical reaction sets up the line of dialogue that follows.

Third, give the line of dialogue.

Then, make sure you pause for reflection.

Taking one of the examples above, you could present the scene like this:

"My son, Jason, had been asking to go to Florida for months. After I reviewed his third quarter grades on line, I called him into the living room.

"What's up, Dad?"

"Jason, I need to talk to you about your grades."

(The speaker creates a worried expression.) "Is there something wrong?"

(The speaker creates a stern look that quickly changes to a huge grin.) "Oh, absolutely ... not! You got straight A's, Kiddo. You know what that means?"

(The speaker creates hopeful, wide-eyed look.) "We're … going … to Florida?"

(The speaker creates an excited expression.) "You bet, son! You lived up to your end of the deal. Now, we're going to live up to ours. We're going next week".

(The speaker creates joyous expression with a huge grin.) "Oh, wow! Thanks, Dad! This is great! I can't wait to tell Ricky."

A key point is that the pauses between the lines allow the audience to feel the scene and give the speaker time to change the facial expressions for each character.

Is the look before the line really that important? You bet. When you can demonstrate the emotions of your characters rather than describe them, audience members feel like they're witnessing the scene live. This helps them capture the emotion of the moment, and they care more about the people involved. That is the power of the "Look Before the Line."

**ACTION STEP:** Review the dialogue in your speech. Look for the lines where emotion is conveyed and where you are describing the feelings rather than showing them. Practice using facial expressions to convey the emotions of each line of dialogue.

**RECOMMENDED RESOURCE:** Re-watch a video you've previously seen by Darren LaCroix. Darren masterfully exhibits the concepts presented in this lesson. For instance, watch the look on his face after he tells his parents he wants to be a comedian. Notice how the change of expression conveys a major shift in emotion. He doesn't need to say a word. To watch this video, visit: http://bit.ly/1nOsAn2.

# Step 41- **Give Voice to Your Characters**

You've read about the speaker who attempts to recreate conversations between characters or tell you what someone else said without conveying character emotions.

"I told my brother, 'I'm really angry that you took my car without asking me.'" Or: "When I heard I had earned a $10,000 bonus, I was so excited!"

Again, most speakers recite these lines in a monotone voice, devoid of inflection or emotion. Their voices don't convey the emotion of a scene.

To help create that "You are there" feeling for the audience, there are three key vocal characteristics you can use. These will put the emotion of the moment into your story. As an added benefit, the listener will gain more insight into the personality of your characters, and they'll feel as if they know each of those characters better.

You'll also learn an exercise you can use to practice for each of these vocal characteristics. To do this most effectively, pick a passage from a favorite story. It's better if the passage has dialogue because you'll be able to practice vocal variations.

**1) Volume.** The first characteristic is volume. Most presenters speak too softly. The loudness or softness of your voice can make a big difference in how the dialogue is interpreted. Scenes take on different meanings based on volume. For instance, excitement tends to require louder speech; sadness usually leads to lower volume.

Saying "I just feel so down about my friends losing their jobs!" in a low tone is more believable than saying it in a loud voice.

Some emotions can create both higher and lower volume. Again, the situation will dictate. Anger is an excellent example. Saying "I said get over here" in a loud voice conveys a much different meaning than saying it in a softer voice.

*Try this exercise:* The Roller Coaster. This is useful to prepare your vocal cords for softer and louder volume. Use a portion of your story and do this exercise. Bring your volume up and down and back up again as you say the words.

**2) Rate.** The second key to deeper connection with your character is the *rate* at which you speak. Like volume, emotion will dictate how fast or slow you say the words. A person who is nervous will usually speak quickly. One who is confused will talk more slowly.

Saying "I'm just so bummed out that I'm not going to get to go on that trip" a bit slowly is more believable than saying it at a faster rate.

As with volume, some emotions can create both quick and slow rates. From the previous example, anger can be expressed both ways. Saying "I said get over here" at a rapid clip conveys a different type of anger than saying it slowly.

*Try this exercise:* Use the Roller Coaster to read your the passage from your story at both slow and fast rates. This will prepare you to vary your speed and adjust according to the needs of the scene.

**3) Tonality.** There's an old saying, "It's not what you say, but how you say it." This refers to the *tonality* aspect of speaking. Your tone dictates the meaning of the words that you speak.

Read the sentence below five times. Each time, place the emphasis on a different word. Consider if the meaning of the sentence changes with each version:

"I didn't say she's alone."

A different emphasis each time creates an entirely different meaning.

*Try this exercise*: Choose one sentence from your story, and change the emphasis of each word. Get a feel for which ones should be emphasized to "sell" the emotion of the line.

Your voice can connect your audience with your characters deeply, or it can alienate the audience. If your delivery doesn't match the mood or emotion of the scene, people will not "buy" your message. They might not consciously know why, but they'll feel as if something isn't quite right with your story.

When you give proper voice to your characters, you'll create an experience that makes a more memorable story, and you will drive your core message deep into the hearts of your listeners.

**ACTION STEP:** Use the exercises in this lesson to better communicate your message through vocal variety. With practice, your volume, rate, and tonality will improve, and the audience will feel as if they know each of the characters in your stories.

**RECOMMENDED RESOURCE:** The audio program entitled "The Perfect Voice" by Roger Love. There are several good programs available on Amazon.com that can strengthen the power of your voice. I like this one because there are various exercises that are easy to use. You'll also pick up useful information about how to take care of your vocal cords. To get your copy, visit: http://voiceplace.com/products/.

# Step 42 - Give Your Audience a Hand

During a recent coaching session, Sarah said, "Michael, what do I do with my hands? I feel self-conscious because I don't know what to do with them."

This is a common question I receive from coaching clients. Unfortunately, too much emphasis is placed on what to do with your hands. Although you'll learn a couple of ideas about this topic in this chapter, you could actually stop this lesson after one sentence:

*"Stop thinking about your hands. Drop them to your sides, and tell your story."*

It's really that simple. However, since you were promised 52 content-rich chapters, let's elaborate.

A common mistake made by presenters is choreographing their hand movements. For instance, a man may say, "reach for the stars" while dramatically pointing his index finger toward the heavens. Or a speaker might talk about a situation that "broke her heart" while clutching her chest to demonstrate her heartache.

These gestures aren't necessary. The audience knows where the stars and your heart are located. These movements become a distraction from your words and can make your speech look staged and fake.

Of course, if it's natural for you in everyday conversation to point to the sky or clutch your chest, don't restrict yourself when telling your story. First and foremost, be yourself.

So, when you begin to think about your hands, your face, or your gestures, ask yourself this question: "Do I make these same movements with my hands, my face, or my body in normal, one-on-one conversation?" If the answer is no, don't do it when you give a speech.

There is one gesture you should avoid even if you use it in day-to-day interactions, however. That is pointing your finger at others. In a word, DON'T. When you point at audiences, you make them feel uncomfortable. Pointing feels accusatory. If you're not sure about this, check your gut reaction the next time a presenter points at you. Does something feel wrong about the gesture?

So, what *can* you do with your hands to emphasize your point? Use an open palm. Hold all of your fingers out, preferably in a sideways gesture. It's still not a good idea to point directly at people, but if you do it with an open palm and all five fingers, it feels less threatening to them.

Generally speaking, just drop your hands to your sides, and let the emotion of the presentation take over. Trust that your hands will do what they normally do, and focus on your material, not your hands. Master this, and you'll be the one giving your audience a big hand.

**ACTION STEP:** Video record your story, and watch it with the sound turned off. Look for movements that seem staged rather than natural. Once you're aware of them, you'll be better able to get rid of them and allow your true nature to shine through.

**RECOMMENDED RESOURCE:** A speech by the great inspirational speaker, Les Brown, entitled "Why People Fail." There are many reasons to watch this video, but keeping in mind the lesson from this chapter, watch how Les easily moves across the stage and uses normal gestures. Nothing about him is staged; his hands do what they would do in a one-on-one conversation. If you also want to take in his message, that won't hurt either. Les is a master of inspiration. To watch this video, visit: http://bit.ly/1oY3NxK.

# Step 43 – The Power of One Simple Facial Gesture

Another tool that isn't used enough is the most basic and powerful facial gesture that you have at your disposal—one that quickly connects you with people from every other background or culture. As you may have guessed, the gesture is *a smile.*

Scientist Andrew Newberg calls a smile "the symbol that was rated with the highest positive emotional content." [xxiv]

You may be thinking, "Michael, why are you taking my valuable time to tell me about smiling? Obviously, people should smile at each other." That's a great point. I'm glad you brought it up. Here's my answer: Because most presenters don't smile very much, if at all.

Think about a speaker you've recently seen. Chances are, that person didn't smile much before s/he spoke and probably didn't smile much during the presentation either. That person probably knew about the need to smile more but still didn't do it. Why? After all, it's a pretty simple act—just lift the corners of your mouth.

There are two main reasons that speakers don't smile. One is nerves. As you've previously read, most presenters are not truly focused on the audience. They're too consumed with questions like, "How do I look?" or "What if I make a mistake?" or "Will I look like a fool out there?" If you're thinking these kinds of things, you feel stress, and stress prevents you from smiling at your audience.

The other reason people don't smile is lack of awareness. Many think that they're giving big smiles when, in fact, they're not. This is a common feeling, not just with smiling, but with gestures in general. Most people think their expressions are much larger than they really are. It isn't uncommon for people to argue when they're told they need to be more expressive . "I did smile!" or "I gave a huge gesture with my arms!" are typical responses I've heard from speakers.

If you're convinced that you're smiling as large as possible, there's one way to find out: Video record yourself.

Chances are, you'll be surprised at how little you smile, laugh, or gesture when you speak. If you're like most people, that's because you're either self-conscious or intimidated when you stand in front of others.

Smiling is important, not just for social etiquette, but because of how you are constructed. Without getting into the details, your brain is wired to respond to a smile as a positive experience. In the article "The science of smiling: A guide to human's most powerful gesture," author Leo Widrich points out:

"According to recent studies, smiling reduces stress that your body and mind feel, similar to getting good sleep. And smiling helps to generate more positive emotions within you. That's why we often feel happier around children—they smile more. On average, they do so 400 times a day. While happy people still smile 40-50 times a day, the average of us only does so 20 times." [xxv]

The latest studies have found that smiling leads to a decrease in the stress-induced hormones that negatively affect our physical and mental health. Why is this important to speakers and storytellers? Because it creates a deeper connection with the audience.

That connection begins, as I've said, with your first impression. Studies show that audiences subliminally decide whether or not they like you within the first 7-30 seconds. That's right, seconds! Since you should do everything possible to connect with people in those precious few moments, why not use the simplest and most effective tool at your disposal?

Just smile.

**ACTION STEP:** Video record your next speech. Watch it with the sound turned off. Look to see if your facial expressions, especially your smile, convey the emotions you feel in each part of your story.

**RECOMMENDED RESOURCE:** The article previously referenced in this lesson, "The science of smiling: A guide to human's most powerful gesture." This article gives you insight into the physiological effects of smiling. You'll have a better understanding of how your brain is impacted by this simple act. To read this article, visit: http://bit.ly/1FTQUtA.

# Step 44 – Listen! The Audience is Talking to You

Is a story a monologue? That's a commonly held belief. It makes sense, right? One person tells a story, and the audience listens. But the reality is that storytelling is a conversation. No, it isn't a conversation in the traditional sense when different people take part vocally, but there's an unspoken dialogue between the speaker and audience members.

Unspoken dialogue refers to the feedback people give you during your story—the expressions on their faces, the sounds they make, and their body movements. Other communication includes their participation in activities, responses during your Question and Answer period, and laughter.

Your communication with an audience actually begins before you speak. It starts when you get to the venue where you're presenting and interact with the first person you meet. Every person is sizing you up, determining whether or not you are approachable and likable. It's important to be pleasant and respectful. Converse with as many people as possible before you step on stage.

As you learned in an earlier lesson, your introduction is a great tool to learn about the temperament of your audience. Watch and listen to their responses as your introduction is read. They'll tell you whether they are alert, bored, ready to laugh, etc. This information can help you adjust your delivery style as you walk to the front of the room.

Once you begin speaking, it's important to pay attention to what people are doing. Watch for the obvious—people checking their cell phones, reading their tablets, or chatting. If several people are doing this, it's up to you to change your delivery to gain their full attention.

In addition to watching them, listen for sounds of disinterest or distraction such as the clearing of throats, rustling of papers, and constant shifting in seats. Again, if several people are doing this, it's up to you to change your delivery to pull them back into your world.

If you're hearing dead silence after you make your key points, laughter after the humorous lines, or sounds like "Hmmm" or "Wow" after your "aha" moments, they've bought into your story.

If you don't have their attention as much as you'd like, the best way to change your delivery is to use silence. Earlier, you learned about the power of the pause. Contrary to popular belief, silence does not compel the audience to become disinterested in your talk. The opposite is true - it creates curiosity. They may be thinking, "What is she going to say next?" or "That poor man! He forgot what he was going to say!" Guess what? It doesn't matter what they're thinking because you've recaptured their attention. You've also had time to adjust your delivery.

Another part of your presentation that will give you feedback is their responses when you ask questions. If they don't participate, make sure you're not confusing them. Keep your questions simple and clear.

This was an issue for me for years. I could often defuse that problem and get them interested by saying, "Well, this is the audience participation part of the program." But that becomes a little clichéd, so be careful.

You can set up your questions with phrases like, "I'm curious what would you think if..." or "If you were in this situation, how would you react?" Those are cues that let them know it's OK to respond.

One other way to improve the communication with your audience is to prepare them to give responses. "Discuss and Debrief" is an activity that creates audience involvement through breaking them up into groups of two or three. Ask them to talk about what they've heard in your talk that they can use immediately. After two or three minutes, bring the group back together, and ask them to share their ideas with everyone.

They're much more likely to open up in a bigger room if they've had the opportunity to discuss their ideas in smaller groups. Their responses will then tell you what parts of your story stuck with them and had the most impact.

Remember that speaking or storytelling is *not* a monologue. It's a two-way dialogue with your audience. Even before you speak, they're communicating with you, and that communication continues until the end of your presentation.

The next time you tell your story, *listen*. The audience is talking to you.

**ACTION STEP**: Test the ideas you learned in this lesson by listening for the auditory responses the audience gives you. Also, watch their actions, and determine if they're engaged or disengaged by your presentation.

**RECOMMENDED RESOURCE:** The audio program, "Connect With Any Audience." This 6-CD set features six World Champion speakers who discuss various tools to connect with your audience. These champions have spoken before audiences of all sizes and makeups all around the world. Their tips are invaluable. To get your copy, visit: http://www.profcs.com/app/?af=750771. Click "Online Store." Then, click "Audio CDs."

# Step 45 - **Call Back to Connect**

Here's a tip to help you quickly connect with your audience, and make them feel as if your speech is tailored just for them.

Use call backs.

Although you may be familiar with these, you may not be aware of how effective they can be.

It's been said "If you want your audience to listen to your message, get 'em laughing." Effectively utilized, call backs create laughter and set the audience up for your main point.

Why do they work so well? Two reasons: 1) When you refer back to a previous speaker[s], it shows you're present, that you're paying attention. 2) Because they are unexpected, call backs catch the audience off guard, and can create big laughs. This will get them on your side.

For example, in a recent speech contest, the main point of my talk was to encourage the audience to stop taking life so seriously. Early in the speech, I asked them to "think about something from everyday life that drives you crazy, r-e-a-l-l-y gets under your skin. It could be a malfunctioning cell phone. Malfunctioning computer. Malfunctioning kid…especially one that wants you to jump off a 105-foot tower."

Since you probably weren't at that contest, you won't understand the humor in that line. The speaker before me, my friend David, gave a great speech about how the words we say to our kids can either encourage them to take risks, or discourage them into not taking action.

During his main story, David recounted a day at a large amusement park and how his 8-year old son wanted to jump off a 105-foot tower, tethered only to a single line, much like a bungee cord. He wanted Dad to join him. David was terrified, and had no interest, but, eventually he acquiesced in order to set an example for his son to take risks.

When I called back to this line from David's speech, the audience roared with laughter. It let them know I was paying attention, and in the moment.

How do you create a great callback? Build it into your speech. Create a 'space' that will allow you to insert a line from another speaker.

In my speech, I knew that most people could relate to malfunctioning cell phones and computers, and the term malfunctioning could be used with a third item/person referred to in a speech before mine. I simply needed to listen closely to other speakers and 'borrow' a line from one of them and insert it into my speech.

Since this was a contest, if I had been the first speaker, I could have referred to frustrating incidents from earlier in the day, such as the lavaliere mic that malfunctioned for 45-minutes during our sound check. This would have also created a big laugh because the audience was frustrated by the delay due to the mic problems. I chose the reference to David's son because I thought it would get a bigger laugh.

There are multiple sources to which you can refer in order to create call backs:

1)  An Event call back - Refer to an incident that occurs at the event where you are speaking. This could involve technology issues like the one mentioned earlier with the microphone, or Power Point.

2)  A Speaker call back - Refer to a line from a previous speaker, as I did with my friend David in the contest mentioned earlier.

3) Presentation - Refer to material presented earlier in your speech. This is the type of call back used by comedians.

Call backs. They are great tools that tell your audience you're in the moment, that you're paying attention to everything happening at their event, and they are a terrific source of laughter.

If you're interested in watching the two speeches referenced earlier, visit: http://bit.ly/1zl0K6e to see David's speech. To see my speech visit: http://bit.ly/1vdZtHG

**ACTION STEP:** Review your story and determine where call backs can be built into it. In my contest video, notice how I structured my ideas about dealing with malfunctioning technology to set up the humorous call back. When you attend other presentations or events, keep your 'radar' on for incidents that can serve as sources of call backs.

**RECOMMENDED RESOURCE:** The audio program *Humor Speaking Secrets* by Craig Valentine. Craig offers 33 keys to creating humor in your stories. One of the areas discussed in great detail is call backs. Craig's material is always content-rich and offers great insight into speaking skills. To get your copy, visit http://www.profcs.com/app/?af=944701.

# Step 46 - Prepare to Be "In the Moment"

Several years ago, Darren LaCroix told me, "Michael, join an improv class. It'll help you be more "in the moment." You'll create a deeper bond with your audience."

Since Darren is a very successful professional speaker, I did what he suggested. I was excited. Having watched improvisational shows like "Whose Line is It Anyway," I had visions of being the star of the class, getting people to laugh uproariously at my hilarious hijinks. Maybe I'd even be discovered and become a comedy star!

It didn't quite work out that way, but what I learned in class taught me how to connect with others on a deeper level, to be more focused on them, and stretch outside my comfort zone.

One person I met in the class was named Joe Boyd. He's an experienced improvisational actor who has since gone on to direct movies. Joe taught me five keys to improv. These also apply to the storytelling world.

**1) Tell a story.** You're probably thinking, "Well, duh, Mike, this is a storytelling book." True. But

Joe's point is that when you tell a story, you're inviting others into your world. That invitation alone is a great connector. It opens the door to sharing a message that can impact your audience.

**2) Fail often, and fail fast**. This is a great *life* lesson. How many people do you know who fret over taking action of any kind and then, when they do, fret over all of the possible outcomes? Joe pointed out that learning and innovation come from taking risks ... and failing. The quicker you get the failure out of the way, the quicker you can make new attempts and get closer to success.

As you develop your story, try different ideas. Change character voices, facial expressions, and attitudes. Adjust words within sentences to see how the meaning and impact change. Test. Fail. Test again. Fail again. Repeat until you reach success.

**3) Agree and accept.** In order for an improv scene to move ahead, the actors must accept the premise given to them no matter how outlandish it may seem. In improv, this can create hilarious situations that leave audiences doubled over in laughter.

In storytelling, however, this can create a major disconnect. Have you ever heard a story that bothered you because it didn't ring true? I once heard one at the World Championship of Public Speaking. The more the speaker talked, the more unbelievable his story became. He lost credibility with many in the audience that day.

When you share your story, it's OK to take slight liberties for the sake of time, but it isn't OK to make up scenarios to create humor or to manipulate audience emotions. The real story will touch the heart of the audience if it's told with integrity.

**4) Heighten and explore.** This is the concept of adding emotion and tension to your story. For example, in an earlier lesson, you read about how director James Cameron heightened the tension in the movie "Titanic" as the water rose in the ship, even though everybody knows the outcome. You can do the same with your story. Create internal tension in key characters, develop a conflict between them, or increase the obstacles faced, and you heighten audience interest.

**5) Play**. This may be the most important tip. Any time you speak, remember this: You're not speaking to a joint session of Congress for a declaration of war. You have the privilege of sharing your story and your ideas with others. Make it fun! Play with the audience. Share a message, but also be entertaining.

Improv isn't just for comedians and actors. It's a great tool that can help you learn to be more in the moment. It helps you practice the unexpected. It triggers creativity. It gives you the experience of making others the hero. And it provides you opportunities to work with a team.

The ultimate benefit is that you become a far better presenter, and your audience gets to be part of a memorable experience that enriches their lives.

**ACTION STEP:** Join an improv group in your area. Go in with the attitude of improvement and fun. Be willing to play, and get outside of your comfort zone.

**RECOMMENDED RESOURCE:** The DVD, "Improv to Improve" by Darren LaCroix. Darren's background as a comedian has provided him with many opportunities to explore improv, and he still practices the craft. This DVD is loaded with exercises that will help you become more spontaneous. Darren is a fantastic teacher, and you'll learn much from him. To get your copy, visit: http://www.profcs.com/app/?af=750771. Click on "Online Store," and then, click "Video DVDs."

# Step 47 - **Rehearsal Mistakes That Can Ruin Your Delivery**

If you want to be a storyteller who is remembered, someone who touches lives and changes people for the better, it's time to use all of the delivery tools you've learned. In other words, *practice!*

To most people, this is a dirty word. It may not always be fun, but it's the one action that separates the great from the mediocre and the unforgettable from the forgettable. In the words of singer Jackson Browne, "You can't hire someone to practice for you."

This point was driven home in Toastmasters 2013 World Championship of Public Speaking. The winner, Presiyan Vasilev, practiced his winning speeches day and night every day for three months. I don't know about the other competitors, but that amount of dedication can make you a champion. To see the end result of his hard work, visit: http://bit.ly/12TwW2q

Before you dive into your practice, however, there are three common mistakes most speakers make.

***Mistake Number One****: They rehearse in front of a mirror.*

Your rehearsal should be as realistic as possible. When you speak to others, will you be looking at yourself in a mirror? No, you will be looking at *them*. Therefore, in your rehearsal, look at your imaginary audience and not at a reflection of yourself.

You can talk to your pets, for example. I used to present many speeches to my dog. I knew I was on the right track when she wagged her tail. If she looked away, there was more work to do.

If you don't have a pet, talk to bushes in the backyard, or pin pictures of people on the wall. Give yourself something to look at.

Another reason to ditch the mirror is that it puts the focus on *you*. By this point, you know that it isn't about you. As Craig Valentine taught me, "You can either look at your own reflection or get the audience to reflect, but you can't do both." Great storytellers choose audience reflection.

***Mistake Number Two****: They always start from the beginning.*

Assume a speaker is preparing a 60-minute speech. She starts rehearsing and, ten minutes in, life interrupts. She stops. Once the interruption is over, she goes back to rehearsing. Where do you think she starts? At the beginning.

She'll continually go back to the beginning, and it will get much more attention than the middle and the conclusion of the story. This has been called a "Slope Speech." It starts off on a high and heads straight downhill.

To avoid your own slope speech, practice in modules. For practice's sake, break your story into at least three parts—the opening, the body, and the conclusion. If possible, break the body into smaller parts as well. That way, if your practice time gets cut, you can just jump into the next module when you have an opportunity to practice again.

***Mistake Number Three:*** *They don't move as they will when they present to an audience.*

Rehearsal isn't just about internalizing your words. It's about the experience of the entire presentation. Some call this "owning the story." You don't think about it; it simply flows out of you.

What many people overlook is that *movement helps internalize the message.* For example, if you're presenting a timeline story, practice delivering different parts of the story in the same timeline fashion you'll give to the audience. If you're addressing a particular character, go to the part of the stage where you want to "anchor" that character.

Doing this will help you remember your points. This is the concept of "muscle memory" that many athletes talk about. Craig Valentine says, "There's something to be said for muscle memory improving your message memory."

When you rehearse, it's important to move like you will on stage. Imagine your audience as if they're sitting in front of you. "See" their reactions, and react to them. Make it as real as possible.

Avoid these three common rehearsal mistakes, and you'll feel as if you're at home the next time you step onto a new stage in front of an unfamiliar audience.

**ACTION STEP:** Rehearse your story using the concepts learned in this lesson. Try one concept for at least three presentations, and then add another. In a short amount of time, you'll be rehearsing in new ways that fully prepare you for your next presentation.

**RECOMMENDED RESOURCE:** The DVD set called Dynamic Delivery Devices, from Craig Valentine. Craig goes in depth to cover many additional ideas that can help you practice and present your story in a world class fashion. These tools helped me make a huge leap in delivering my speeches and stories. Visit <u>CraigValentine.com</u>. Click 'Speaking Products' tab. Scroll down to 'Dynamic Delivery Devices 3-DVD set for Speakers'

# Step 48 - **Clear as Mud**

In the real estate world, the most important part of selling a home is *location, location, location.* In the storytelling world, the most important aspect is *clarity, clarity, clarity.*

This subject was touched upon in a previous lesson, and it bears repeating in more detail. In any type of communication, clarity is critical to ensuring that the message you deliver is received by the other persons just as you intended. In storytelling, your walk-away message and the next step must be crystal clear if you want to leave a lasting impact on your audience. Unfortunately, far too many presenters are as clear as mud.

Is it the audience's fault? They just don't "get it," right?

No, the problem lies in a concept called "The Curse of Knowledge." This term was described in the book, *Made to Stick*, by Chip and Dan Heath. [xxvi] It means that it's difficult to communicate when you know a fact that someone else doesn't. This disconnect creates communication problems between people.

To help you understand this, try the following exercise. Think of a song that everyone knows.

Then, tap the rhythm of that song out on a desktop, and ask another person to guess the name of the song. ("Happy Birthday" works well.) You'll find that most people don't have a clue what song you're tapping out. All they hear is a random rhythm.

How is it that someone couldn't understand such a simple and universally known song? When you don't know the title of the song, you have no reference point. Once you learn the name of the song, you can match the melody to the tapping.

What does this have to do with storytelling? When you have an idea in your head, *you* understand it because it's clear in your mind. But you have to tie your story around a central message and express it clearly, or your audience, in essence, will hear a series of meaningless taps.

How can you clarify your message to others? Try this suggestion from my fellow Certified World Class Speaking Coach, Bob Mohl. Present your story to a group, and a week later, contact each of the people who heard your story. Ask them these three questions:

1. *What do you remember?*
2. *What was the point of the story?*
3. *What was funny?*

A word of warning: The responses may astound you. What you think is memorable often isn't. The point you think you're making is frequently *not* what people take away. Parts you think are funny may not be to others.

This exercise can be one of the most valuable tools you use to improve your story and your impact on an audience. The feedback is invaluable. If people can't remember key points a week later, your story is not resonating. When your message and next step are clear, your story will be remembered. People will think about its implications long after you speak, and you will avoid the curse of being "clear as mud."

**ACTION STEP:** Use the three follow-up questions discussed in this week's lesson. Whenever you sense that your audience is not clear about your message, think about the tapping exercise and upon whom the responsibility lies for the clarity of your message. Use the feedback from the three questions to eliminate confusing or forgettable parts of your story.

**RECOMMENDED RESOURCE:** The book, *Wake 'em Up Business Presentations*, by Tom Antion. Tom is a highly successful speaker and internet entrepreneur who has been entertaining audiences for over 25 years. One of Tom's strengths is the clarity of his messages. When he speaks or presents his internet workshops, you walk away knowing exactly what his subject matter is. In this book, he offers scores of ideas on humor, audience involvement, and methods to develop crystal clear messages, create energy and maintain audience interest. To get your copy, visit: http://amzn.to/1zmPvti.

# Step 49 - **Record and Replay**

What is the most important tool you have to quickly improve your stories? Feedback from others? Yes, that's helpful, but it's limited because you can't see what others see when they give you those evaluations.

As you've previously heard, the best feedback tools you have are video and audio recordings. You probably don't like how you look or sound on these recordings, but remember the words of my friend Darren LaCroix: "Too bad. WE had to listen!"

This is a really funny response, but there's some truth to it. The fastest road to improvement is to watch and listen to yourself. When you get feedback from others and can then review the recordings, you'll have a much better understanding of the evaluations you receive.

For example, someone might tell me, "Michael, if you would have drawn out that pause a couple more seconds and not been smiling when the guy threatened you with the knife, it would've been more believable."

My reaction might be, "I *did* pause a long time!" or "I wasn't smiling!" When I go back and watch the video, though, and see that I did both, the feedback has more meaning.

Try watching the video with the sound turned off, and then watch it at two times the normal speed. This helps you focus on the visual aspect of your presentation. Distracting mannerisms or movements that seem unnatural become more apparent when you review the videos in this manner.

Here are five specific aspects of your video and audio recordings to watch and listen for:

**1) Pauses.** By now, you've probably figured out that this is one of my favorite speaking topics. Silence is where your key points are made, where tension is built, and where humor takes hold. Use a stopwatch to time your pauses at the most important parts of your story. Whatever your time is, *add to it*. Stretch yourself. Become one of the rare, handful of speakers who properly uses the pause to enhance your stories.

**2) Audience reaction.** Listen to determine if the audience is reacting the way you anticipated. Are they laughing at humorous lines? Are they participating when you ask? Is there silence at poignant or important moments?

Listen to the recording twice. The second time, focus on sounds from the audience. Do you hear chatter, papers rustling, coughing, or other noises? These are an indication that the audience isn't 100% engaged. They're telling you that you need to adjust your material or your delivery.

If you hear nothing, you're on the right path. This is a case where silence is golden.

**3) Clarity.** Is your message consistent? Does the story support the message? Are you giving too much information? Are you clear?

**4) Voice.** Does your voice match the emotion of the characters and the situations? This is a common problem. A speaker may say that she's "really angry" in a low, slow tone, maybe even with a hint of a smile. Another may tell you that he was "really happy" with little energy and a stoic expression on his face. Clearly, their voices and expressions don't reflect their words. The audience may not be conscious of these contradictions, but they get a sense that something doesn't feel right when you present in this way. Make sure your voice properly represents the mood of the moment and the characters.

**5) Body and energy.** In addition to voice, many speakers send mixed messages with their body and energy. If you're sharing an exciting moment, let your body and face represent this. If the situation is sad or fearful, show that, too.

In Step 42, you were taught to not focus on creating gestures, to allow them flow out of you. One additional idea to consider is to not purposely 'hold back' - don't be so self-conscious that you artificially restrict movements that you normally make.

I recently saw a speaker who was talking about spreading her message all around the world. She held her arms less than 12 inches apart as she said this. Not a gesture that connotes such a wide-reaching message. Again, this is subtle, and as an audience member you may not consciously think about the incongruity. All you know is that something doesn't feel right when you see that inconsistency.

If you're serious about becoming better and doing it faster, the best tools at your disposal are audio and video recordings. Thanks to the proliferation of smart phones, you have no more excuses to not record yourself. Use the tips in this lesson, and you'll realize the quickest possible growth.

**ACTION STEP:** Record. Record. Record. This is not a broken tape. Ask for written evaluations of the stories you record. With those evaluations in hand, watch and listen. You will then be able to make sense of the evaluations.

**RECOMMENDED RESOURCE:** You may have guessed it: Your own recordings are your resource for this chapter. All of the ideas you've gotten from this book and other speakers and storytellers are only valuable if you use them. Focus your efforts from this lesson on your own work. This is also a great measuring stick to see how far you've come in 50 lessons.

# Step 50 - Create Curiosity BEFORE You Speak

*"Our next speaker, John Smith, is a highly accomplished financial planner. He started in the business at age 25, and within three years, was a President's Council qualifier. He has been a leading producer for our company for the last 17 years. In that time, he has built two successful agencies, and the sales program he and his team created has improved the annual revenues of our firm 22% every year for the past decade. Please help me welcome Mr. John Smith."*

Does that speech introduction sound familiar? It isn't an uncommon type of introduction.

Is there anything wrong with it? No. Are the speaker's credentials impressive? Definitely. Are his accomplishments something to aspire to? Maybe. Now, the important question. Is his introduction relatable? Probably not.

When you hear that type of introduction, what do you think? If you're like most people, you probably think "That's impressive. This guy has done a lot. I'm not sure I could do that, though."

What's worse, as impressive as those achievements are, they don't seem real. People typically don't accomplish great feats without some kind of struggle, but you didn't hear about those struggles in the introduction.

This type of introduction alienates the audience before you say a word, and many speakers don't realize they're creating a barrier with their self-centered introductions.

You can more quickly connect with an audience by sharing your struggles before you tell them how great you are. What is a better way to develop a bond and interest in what you have to say?

Use the introduction to arouse curiosity and interest in your subject, and come across as similar to your audience. How do you do this? Use the following steps to create a killer introduction:

1. Make your first sentence about **the audience.**
2. Promise a benefit **they** will receive.
3. Use only your **relevant** credentials.
4. Wherever possible, turn everything about *you* into **something about *them.***

Let's rework that introduction and make it more audience-centered:

*"Is it possible that you could become a top producer despite no sales background? What if you failed miserably and nearly washed out of the business before age 27? Our next speaker proves that yes, you can overcome struggles and succeed in this business. John Smith has used the processes and sales tools you are about to learn to achieve Presidents Council 17 times. When you put these tools into practice, you will be able to qualify prospective clients more quickly, develop meaningful and trusting relationships with them, and double your number of appointments in the next 12 months. Additionally, your organization can realize 22% annual increases in sales like John's team has each year for the past decade. He believes that if he can do this, so can you. You simply need to learn and use the lessons his mentors have taught him. Please help me welcome Mr. John Smith."*

Who is the focus in that introduction? Clearly, it's the audience. You've heard a quick background about some of John's early struggles, including that he learned tools from his mentors and that he's had great success since then.

John doesn't take credit for his ideas; his mentors get the credit. It's only after you've heard about his struggles that you hear about his relevant success. And it's OK to tell them at that point because it gives John credibility.

Can you see the difference? Don't you feel more connected to John and want to learn how he turned his situation around? Change the focus of your introduction, and you change the audience attitude toward you before you even speak.

One other way to use your introduction is to test the humor and energy level of your audience. Darren LaCroix is a master at using this strategy. He includes a couple of humorous lines in each of his introductions.

As it is read, Darren listens to the audience responses. If there's uproarious laughter, he knows he can be a little more humorous and energetic in his opening. If there is a muted response or no response, he knows he needs to be a little more low-key and not quite so funny, at least until the audience is warmed up and he's connected with them.

Focusing on the benefits to the audience and gauging their humor and energy level are the strengths of a properly structured introduction. Create your own killer introduction, and you'll create curiosity before you say a word.

**ACTION STEP:** Create the initial draft of your introduction. Remember to use the four-step process:

1. Make the first sentence about them.
2. Make a promise with a specific benefit to the audience.
3. Use only your relevant credentials.
4. Wherever possible, turn everything about *you* into something about *them*.

**RECOMMENDED RESOURCE:** The book, *Talk Like TED,* by Carmine Gallo. Mr. Gallo is the author of several outstanding books on the art of public speaking. In this work, he delves into nine keys to creating and delivering a memorable TED talk. He also offers links to the videos he reviews so that you, too, can see the various skills he highlights. To get your copy, visit: http://amzn.to/1yrQcyK.

# Step 51 - **Lessons From a Eulogy**

Ryan stood before the congregation, fighting to control his emotions. He unfolded his carefully handwritten eulogy.

"I'm here to tell you about my grandpa, my hero. My first memories of him are when I was five ... years old."

After a long pause, he mumbled, "I can't do this." He started to fold that handwritten paper. There wasn't a sound in the church. He began to step away. Then, he stopped. After a long pause, he stepped back to the lectern, unfolded the paper, and picked up where he left off.

After five minutes of speaking, he said his final words, folded his paper, slipped it into his pocket, and walked back to his pew and sat down.

His cousin, Leah, then stepped up to the lectern. Her eulogy was filled with humorous stories about her grandpa. She painted such vivid pictures that I could recall memories I experienced in their grandfather's house, and I hadn't been there in over 20 years.

Leah's eulogy was the perfect match for Ryan's. His was filled with lessons learned, love and respect for his grandfather, and his emotions were raw and unchecked. Leah's was filled with humor, love and respect for her grandfather, and her emotions were kept in check.

It was one of the most heartfelt and real pair of presentations I've ever heard.

As a speaker and coach, I was reminded that day of these important lessons:

- When you speak with real emotion, you create a deep connection with others. It's a shared experience because it's authentic.

- Two people with the same grandfather, feeling similar emotions about him, used different methods of expressing their love and grief. One was not better than the other.

- By speaking from their hearts and sharing their experiences and perspectives, Ryan and Leah provided more depth and insight into their grandfather.

These were not two professional speakers or storytellers. They were simply two people who shared their thoughts and feelings, without shame and embarrassment, about a man they loved.

What can *you* take away from this experience?

**1) When sharing a story, it's OK to show emotion.** Shedding tears or laughing is appropriate, as long as it doesn't overwhelm your presentation. If you find that you're too overcome with emotion when sharing a story, it's too soon to tell it to an audience. Never use the stage for your own therapy.

Also, never use your emotions to manipulate the audience's emotions. I've seen speakers who cry "on cue" in the same moment every time they share the same story. If you're genuinely moved by a situation, you're not going to cry at the exact same spot for the same length of time every time you tell it. People can sense insincerity.

**2) Your perspective is an important addition to any story.** Just as Ryan shared his grief through tears and Leah shared hers through laughs, you can offer a unique view of other people or incidents. This gives a more complete picture of that person or situation.

**3) You may generate a response you didn't expect.** When Leah finished speaking, her Uncle Rudy stood up and applauded. It was a spur-of-the-moment reaction, and it was beautiful. (The priest didn't think so, but that was his problem.) Rudy's spontaneous response was one of genuine appreciation for words that paid tribute to his father.

As you prepare your story, accept that emotional parts of it may have an impact on you. When this happens, stay in the moment. Let the emotion wash through you. Do not apologize. Your audience will be drawn closer to you because you're allowing yourself to be open and vulnerable.

**ACTION STEP:** Practice and internalize your speech. When you know your material, you're much more likely to be aware of audience reactions. When you know your material well, your emotions will flow through you, and when you and your audience are in synch emotionally, you can live in the moment. You can then present a story that people will remember.

**RECOMMENDED RESOURCE:** The book, *Confessions of a Public Speaker,* by Scott Berkun. Mr. Berkun offers a real world view of the challenges of speaking and storytelling. He has a witty and energetic style that keeps you turning the pages, and his experiences can help you save time

and embarrassment. To get your copy, visit:
http://amzn.to/1nGocEg.

# Step 52 - Avoid These 11 Mistakes That Can Kill Your Story

As we near the end of the book, this is a great time to review a list of common mistakes that we've covered that hurt most storytellers. Avoiding them can cut years off of your learning curve. Keep this list nearby as you prepare your stories.

**11 common speaker mistakes:**

**Mistake #1:** *They speak in narration and don't use dialogue.* The majority of speakers narrate their stories. This makes them sound like reporters. A small number of people speak almost entirely in dialogue, which makes them sound more like actors in a stage play.

Overcome this mistake by using a mixture of both. Ideally, use narration of the story to set up the dialogue.

**Mistake #2:** *They don't describe their characters effectively.* Most storytellers don't give enough of a description of their characters. This lack of information creates too many questions in the minds of the audience, distracting them from the story. On the other hand, some speakers give too many details, which makes them sound as if they're reciting a novel.

Remember that when characters can be seen and heard, they are more relatable. The best way to describe them is through dialogue. Effectively done, this can quickly provide pertinent description and keep the audience engaged.

**Mistake #3:** *They don't establish conflict early in the story.* Remember that conflict is the hook. The quicker you introduce the conflict, the quicker you create audience interest.

**Mistake #4:** *They don't escalate the conflict.* It isn't enough to just establish conflict; it's also important to escalate it to the point where it needs to be resolved. For maximum effect, the escalation must be gradual. Remember the film, "Titanic." After the ship hit the iceberg, there would have been tragedy but no tension if it had immediately sunk to the ocean bottom. If it had taken on a little water but stayed afloat for days with plenty of time for all passengers to be rescued, there also would have been no tension.

Properly escalated, tension can set the audience up. And they want to know the tools that were used to solve that conflict.

**Mistake #5:** *They don't explain the cure.* The cure is the scene where the character goes through an "aha" moment. This is the change the audience wants to experience. Properly done, this sets them up for an explanation of that change.

**Mistake #6:** *They don't show the change after the cure.* Once you share the cure for the conflict, it's critical to show how the character changed as a result. If your character doesn't experience a change, your story won't resonate or be remembered. To quote Craig Valentine, "If you take us through the problem, take us through the payoff." Far too many storytellers leave out the benefit of the change and leave their audiences wondering about the purpose of the story.

*Mistake #7:* *They make themselves the hero.* Remember, when you lift yourself up, you let others down. Too many speakers tell stories in which they have all the answers to the problems they face. Unfortunately, audiences don't connect with speakers who come across as special or have all the answers.

Give credit to others who passed on wisdom or solutions to you. This enables you to stay on the same level as your audience and will deepen your bond with them.

**Mistake #8:** *They don't use character reactions to enhance the emotion of the story.* To quote Darren LaCroix, "It's often the look before and after the line that makes the line work." Very few speakers understand this. They feel that they need to fill up their speaking time with words.

When you show a character's reaction to a situation or what was said, the audience will see and feel your story and become more involved.

**Mistake #9:** *They don't get into their story quickly.* Remember to *Arrive Late, Leave Early.* Most speakers take too much time to set up their story. If you inundate the audience with extraneous details, they will lose interest and mentally check out. Get to the key parts of your story as quickly as possible.

**Mistake #10:** *Early in their stories, they don't give the audience an idea of the benefit they're about to receive.* If you don't tell the audience at the beginning what they're going to get, they won't want to go on the journey with you.

In the opening of their stories, far too many presenters give in-depth background information that doesn't add to their message. It's never good for your audience to think, "What in the world does this have to do with me?"

**Mistake #11:** *They speak the way they write.* A good story is like a good conversation, just with more people involved. Remember the words of Rob Friedman, "Writing should not be for the page, but for the ear." [xxvii] Because most speakers write their stories out, they have a tendency to speak the way they write. If you want to stand out, turn this formula around.

As you go through your story, ask yourself one question: "Do I talk like this in everyday conversation?" Don't use words in your stories that you don't use in everyday life. You'll seem insincere and lack authenticity.

When you use the same language in your stories that you use in everyday life, the audience gets the real version of you.

**ACTION STEP:** Review your story and your recordings. I know you've been recording each of your speeches since you read about that recommendation, haven't you? Determine if you're making any of the 11 mistakes in this chapter. Use this as a checklist to go over each of your stories.

**RECOMMENDED RESOURCE:** The CD series, "The Hero's 2 Journeys" by Michael Hague and Christopher Vogler. Mr. Hague and Mr. Vogler are highly regarded and sought-after

Hollywood screenwriting consultants. These audios are more detailed than other resource recommended in this course. They offer great insight into key aspects of story creation, such as character emotions, plot development, and how to create a "rooting" interest in your characters. To get your copy, visit: http://amzn.to/1zeTZm8.

# A Final Word

You've made it through all 52 lessons! In this book, you've journeyed into a world of moviemakers, comedians, professional speakers, screenwriters, presidents, world champions, writers, academics, sales professionals, legendary business leaders, and personal development experts. Despite their different vocations and varied backgrounds, these remarkable people have one skill in common: **They are master storytellers.**

If you've done the exercises and used just a few of the recommended resources, *your* ability to tell stories is light years ahead of where it was when you started this book. You now know more than many professional speakers and writers about creating a story that grabs and keeps audience attention and interest.

Although this part of our journey together is ended, this isn't a conclusion. I encourage you to go back through these lessons. In every program or course I've taken, I've gotten the most long-lasting impact after reviewing that material at least three times.

The next time you read this book, you'll pick up ideas you missed the first time. This program was designed for you to go back time and time again, and to help you deepen your understanding each time you review it.

You are strongly encouraged to invest in the resources recommended after each lesson. Every single one has had an impact on how I develop and deliver stories and speeches.

The most important advice I can leave you with is to put these ideas to use. Far too many people fall short of success because they don't take focused, deliberate action. Susan Cain makes this point in her book, *Quiet: The Power of Introverts in a World that Can't Stop Talking.* Ms. Cain points out that "When you practice deliberately, you identify the tasks or knowledge that are just out of your reach, strive to upgrade your performance, monitor your progress, and revise accordingly." [xxviii]

**If you are willing to engage in this type of work, you will leap ahead of at least 90% of all other speakers and storytellers.**

Every tip you've read in this book is one that my mentors and I have tested. We have also "failed" many times in our attempts, but we haven't actually viewed them as failures. We just see it as learning what doesn't work.

If you're like some people, you want to sulk and pout and feel sorry for yourself. I've felt that way at times - everyone has. Just don't stay in that emotional frame of mind. Get up and try again. Sometimes you'll succeed, and sometimes you won't. Either way, you're growing because you're learning. Keep doing what works well, and discard what doesn't.

In closing, I have one request: Please stay in touch. Let me know which of these tips is working for you and how they're helping. I'd love to know your unique perspective about storytelling. I'm continually studying the craft and can never learn too much.

I can't leave you, however, without offering two more resources. The first is the program *Stand Up, Stand Out! Home Study Course*. This series will teach you how to develop and deliver a *Stand OUT!* speech that increases your *impact, influence,* and *income*.

The lessons I've learned from Hall of Fame and World Champion speakers since 2001 have been compacted into this program. When you complete this Home Study workshop, you'll have a compelling speech that can be delivered in a five-minute networking session, a 20-minute Chamber talk, or a half-day workshop. You'll leave people wanting to hear more and seeking you out to do business.

Because of your investment in this book, you are eligible for a 50% discount on the course. Your discount code for this is **52BooksTips50%**. Type this into the *Coupon Code* box of the Checkout page. Please don't share this with anyone else; it's your reward for your commitment to self-improvement!

For more information about this program, feel free to visit the Online Store at <u>SpeakingCPR.com</u>.

The other recommended resource is a three-minute video called "The Power of Giving" that captures the essence of storytelling and the lessons you've learned in this book. It will pique your interest, move you emotionally, and touch your heart. Watch it a couple of times for the effect, and then go back to review it and pick out the most important storytelling elements. It's a model for what a great story *can* be. Here is the link: http://bit.ly/1sp56lq.

And it wouldn't hurt to keep a couple of tissues nearby when you watch it.

It is my deepest hope that our journey together has provided you with tools that enable you to stretch outside your comfort zone, increase your confidence in sharing your stories, and help you succeed at a level higher than before - perhaps even greater than you've ever thought possible.

Always remember that **you** have a story that **someone** needs to hear.

# About the Author

Michael R. Davis believes that public speaking is the most important business skill you can develop. It can profoundly impact your career growth and personal development. He should know, because it happened to him.

As a 6-year old child, he suffered an embarrassing experience that, for 25 years, keep him from *voluntarily* standing before others and speaking. At age 31, his job as a financial planner was in jeopardy because his job required that he present public financial planning workshops. Unless he learned to control his anxiety and learn how to speak well, he could lose his job. After picking up the tools to control his nerves, he discovered he had an affinity for giving speeches, and coaching others to become more effective presenters.

He has been speaking professionally since 2001. He is an avid student of the art of public speaking and storytelling. He has worked closely with Hall of Fame and World Champion speakers, learning how to craft and deliver presentations that capture audience attention, keep them on the edge of their seats, and compel them to take action. His specialty is the crafting and delivery of stories.

He is a contributing author to three books about speaking and marketing:

The Amazon #1 best-selling **World Class Speaking in Action** (2014 - Morgan James Publishing).

**Mastering Your Connections** (2013 - Greydon Press).

**Go Ahead and Laugh:** *A Serious Guide to Humor* (2012 - CreateSpace Independent Publishing Platform).

In 2011, Michael earned the designation of *Certified World Class Speaking Coach* from World Champion speaker Craig Valentine and internet marketing expert Mitch Meyerson.

He has also developed CD/Mp3 and video educational tools focused on improving your public speaking and storytelling skills. These include *Stand Up, Stand OUT!* **Home Study Course,** and *Panic to Power.* His energetic and content-rich speaking workshops are in high demand and leave attendees with tools and processes that take their speaking abilities to a higher level.

Michael has taught presentation skills at companies including General Electric, Johnson & Johnson, and Procter and Gamble.

He continually improves his knowledge of public speaking with research and study of leading industry experts, and attendance at events hosted by speaking-oriented organizations like the National Speakers Association and Toastmasters International.

His goal to teach professionals how to use public speaking skills to free up their time, increase their income, advance their careers faster, become better known in their industries and have more fun when they speak (yes, it IS possible to have fun when you give a speech!).

Michael attended the University of Cincinnati, and is a 26-year veteran of the financial services industry. He currently lives in Blue Ash, Ohio.

For more information about Michael Davis and his company, Speaking CPR, visit **SpeakingCPR.com**.

# Acknowledgements

"If I have seen further than others, it is by standing upon the shoulders of giants."
Isaac Newton

When I walked into my first Toastmasters meeting in May, 1994, I had no idea my life was about to take a new direction. The people I have met because of my association with that organization are **the** reason I am able to write this book.

Acknowledging all of the people who have impacted me from both Toastmasters and the National Speakers Association would fill a book. However, there are some individuals I must specifically thank, each a giant in my eyes. They have laid the foundation for my public speaking and storytelling knowledge.

**World Champions of Public Speaking**: Ryan Avery, David Brooks, Mark Brown, Randy Harvey, Vikas Jhingran, Jim Key, Darren LaCroix, Lance Miller, Duane Smith, Ed Tate, Craig Valentine, and Otis Williams.

Although you've taught me the skills it takes to be a world class speaker; the more important lessons you've taught are about what it takes to be a world class person - to be willing to share your gifts and knowledge and give back. You have each made me a better man with your example, friendship and counsel.

To the great lady of speaking, Ms. Patricia Fripp, and the incomparable Les Brown, who, from a distance have taught me what it means to be a speaker who touches the heart and inspires others to take action. Thank you.

To my friend and coach Duane Plapp, for asking me a very simple question in early 2014: "Why haven't you turned your 52 Storytelling Tips into a Book?" Thanks to your question, that book is now a reality.

One final thank you to the woman who has walked this journey with me, who helped me re-discover the courage and persistence to complete this work. Thank you, Linda, for being the best partner a man could ask for and for encouraging me to keep pushing forward. I love you.

# Appendix

## The 12 *Stand OUT!* Storytelling Competencies

*On a scale of 1 to 10 (1 being least effective and 10 being as effective as possible), rate your skills in each of the following areas:*

1.  *Storytelling:* How well do you use stories to support your main message and "sell" your benefits to an audience? **Your rating** _____

2.  *Selling:* How good are you at selling ideas, products, or services to an audience? **Your rating** _____

3.  *Process Driven:* How well do you give credit to the processes, formulas, or systems you promote, rather than building yourself up? **Your rating** _____

4.  *Next Steps:* How effective are you at providing one specific next step for your audience to take? **Your rating** _____

5.  *Anchor-Driven:* How effectively do you use Anchors (stories, analogies, acronyms, activities, videos, etc.) to make your points more memorable? **Your rating** _____

6.  *Begin with a Bang:* How effectively do you use the first 30 seconds of your presentation to grab your audience's attention and make them want to hear more? **Your rating** _____

7.  *Succinct:* How well do you get to the point and not overwhelm your audience with too much information? **Your rating** _____

8.  *You-Focused:* How much do you focus on the audience with "You-focused" statements versus "I-focused" statements? **Your rating** _____

9.  *Dynamic:* Rate your enthusiasm, energy, and ability to connect with your audience when you present your story. **Your rating** _____

10. *Involvement:* How well do you get audience involvement in your presentation from start to finish? **Your rating** _____

11. *Staging:* How effectively do you use your entire speaking area to support your message? **Your rating**

   _____

12. *Research Driven:* How well do you research your audiences before you present and assess their involvement with you throughout your presentation? **Your rating** _____

# Footnotes

1. Patricia Fripp. "Your audience will not remember what you say, but what they see in their minds. Tell stories." www.FRIPP.com. ABOUT page. MORE ABOUT FRIPP section. FRIPPICISMS section. COMMUNICATIONS quotes. Accessed 13 Dec. 2014.

2. Rory Vaden (@rory_vaden), "Mistakes are proof that you're trying." 29 Aug, 2014, 12:00pm tweet

3. Paul Smith, *Lead with a Story*, (New York: AMACOM, 2012), p. 11-12.

4. Evelyn Clark, original findings from the *Teaching Firm Where Productive Work and Learning Converge* (Newton, MA: The Center for Workplace Development, 1998). Clark's commentary is from the Center for Workplace Development, *Around the Corporate Campfire: How great Leaders Use Stories to Inspire Success* (Sevierville, TN: Insight Publishing, 2004) p. 215

5. Margaret Parkin, *Tales for Change: Using Storytelling to Develop People and Organizations* (London: Kogan Page, 2004) p. 37

6. Mary Wacker and Lori Silverman, *Stories Trainers Tell: 55 Ready-to-Use Stories to Make Training Stick* (San Francisco: Jossey-Bass Pfeiffer, 203), p xxv.

7. Annette Simmons, *Whoever Tells the Best Story Wins: How to Use Your Own Stories to Communicate with Power and Impact* (New York: AMACOM, 2007), p 28.

8. David Armstrong, *Managing by Storying Around: A New Method of Leadership* (NEw York: Doubleday Currency, 1992), p. 13.

9. Randy Harvey and Ryan Avery, *How to Be a Speaker* CD program, 2014

10. Randy Harvey, *Public Speaking 101: Messages That Matter* (Eugene, Oregon: Fatdad Publishing, 2013), p. 9.

11. David Brooks, *Speaking Secrets of the Champions* CD program, 2005.

12. Robert McKee, "Given the choice between trivial material brilliantly told versus profound material badly told, an audience will always choose the trivial told brilliantly." www.GoodReads.com. Robert McKee quotes page. Accessed 13 Dec. 2014.

13. Michael McKinley, "Audiences have seen smooth; they've seen slick. Don't fake who you are. When giving speeches, you can work so hard on the WHAT that you forget the WHO, which is you. The audience wants to see your vulnerability and what you've done with your failures. They want you to offer hope that they too can overcome whatever obstacles come their way." www.SpeakingSecrets.net. Archive for Category Uncategorized. Larry Wilson - Failure Offers Hope section. Accessed 13 Dec. 2014.

14. Jim Rohn, "There are two types of pain you will go through in life, the pain of discipline and the pain of regret. Discipline weighs ounces while regret weighs tonnes." www.GoodReads.com. Jim Rohn quotes page. Accessed 13 Dec. 2014.

15. Smith, *Lead with a Story,* p. 55.

16. Smith, *Lead with a Story,* p. 55.

17. Rob Friedman, "Writing should not be for the page, but for the ear," as quoted by Patricia Fripp on www.FRIPP.com. BLOG page. Blog entitled *Executive Speech Coach and How to Write a Speech.* Accessed 14 Dec. 2014.

18. William Goldman, *Adventures in the Screen Trade* (New York: Warner Books, 1983)

19. Patricia Fripp, *"Your audience will forgive you for almost anything – except being boring."* www.Fripp.com. BLOG page. Blog entitled *'What You Can Do When Your Audience Tunes Out.'* Accessed 14 Dec. 2014.

20. Patricia Fripp, *"Last Words Linger"* www.Fripp.com. BLOG page. Blog entitled *'Last Words Linger – Sales Presentation Tip.'* Accessed 14 Dec. 2014.

21. Patricia Fripp, *"The first thirty seconds have the most impact. Don't waste these precious seconds with "Ladies and Gentlemen" or a weather report. Come out punching with a startling statement, quote, or story"* www.Fripp.com. BLOG page. Article entitled *'10 Tips for Public Speaking from Executive Speech Coach Patricia Fripp.'* Accessed 14 Dec. 2014.

22. Darren LaCroix, "Winning Toastmasters Motivational Speeches by World Champion Darren LaCroix at NSA" Online video clip. *You Tube.* You Tube, 23 June 2010.

23. Darren LaCroix. www.DarrenLaCroix.com. BLOG page. Stage Time Articles Page. Article *'STAGE TIME: What you DO & THINK 5 minutes before a presentation will make it or break it. The Simple Solution!'* Accessed 14 Dec. 2014.

24. Andrew Newberg, quoted in the article, *'The Science of Smiling: A Guide to Human's Most Powerful Gesture'* written by Leo Willrich. www.blog.bufferapp.com. SOCIAL MEDIA page. Blog posted 9 April 2013. Accessed 14 Dec. 2014.

25. Willrich, *'The Science of Smiling: A Guide to Human's Most Powerful Gesture.'* Blog posted 9 April 2013.

26. Chip and Dan Heath, *Made to Stick,* (New York: Random House, 2007) p. 19-21

27. Rob Friedman, "Writing should not be for the page, but for the ear," as quoted by Patricia Fripp on www.FRIPP.com. BLOG page. Blog entitled *Executive Speech Coach and How to Write a Speech*. Accessed 14 Dec. 2014.

28. Susan Cain, *Quiet:The Power of Introverts in a World that Can't Stop Talking*, (New York: Random House, 2012) p. 81

CPSIA information can be obtained
at www.ICGtesting.com
Printed in the USA
LVHW080740250919
631984LV00030B/819/P